HARD: Building Your Inner Citadel

Published by Root Astro Publishing, Belleair, Florida.

the application of information contained in this book, including but not limited to special, incidental, consequential, or other damages.

Further, readers should be aware that websites listed in this work may have changed or disappeared from the internet.

Library of Congress Control Number:2026909255

ISBN 979-8-9956591-0-5 (ebook)

ISBN 979-8-9956591-1-2 (paperback)

First published in the United States of America, 2026

CONTENTS

DEDICATION

For my Mum.

The fearless leader who taught me how to be the rescue.

ACKNOWLEDGEMENTS

Some debts can't be repaid. They can only be acknowledged.

To my mum: You were the first person who showed me what it looks like to lead without flinching. This book is, at its core, your lesson, written long.

To my father: You taught me to stand my ground.

To my daughters & granddaughter: you are the reason the work matters.

To my wife: You hold the ground. That's not a small thing. Grateful none of this gets built alone.

To my dear friends: The ones who showed up, checked in, and didn't ask too many questions when I disappeared into the desert. You know who you are.

To everyone who believes that hardship is not the enemy of growth but the engine of it: this book is for you.

PROCEEDS

The proceeds of this book will be donated to registered children's charities that the author supports. At the time of writing, these include Baby Zone, https://babyzone.org.uk/, and New Yorkers for Children, https://www.newyorkersforchildren.org/.

Both charities support transformational redirection into better futures through creating safe spaces & education.

INTRODUCTION - WHY HARD IS THE ANSWER

In October 2025, at mile 205 of a 240-mile race through the Utah desert, I sat down on a rock and had a conversation with myself that I had been avoiding for two years.

Not a motivational conversation. Not a breakthrough moment with a swelling soundtrack. A reckoning. The kind that only arrives when you have stripped away everything that isn't essential, the devices, the meetings, the deals, the comfortable performances of competence, and the only thing left is you, a headlamp, and 35 miles of darkness.

I finished the Moab 240. And I came back a different person. Not because I suffered. Because I chose to, deliberately, with full understanding of the cost. That choice, structured, bounded, intentional, is what this book is about.

> *This book does not argue that suffering is virtuous. It argues that deliberately chosen hardship, with a purpose and a finish line, does something to a person that comfort cannot undo.*

What Is Actually Breaking

Modern life has been engineered to remove friction. Every inconvenience smoothed, every wait eliminated, every discomfort preempted by an algorithm that already knows what you want before you've decided. We call this progress. It may be. But it carries a tax we have not been honest about.

Attention is the first casualty. When nothing requires sustained effort, the capacity for sustained effort quietly atrophies. Not with any announcement, just with a gradual shortening of the window before the mind drifts away. Then judgment. Then resilience. Then, most corrosively, integrity: the alignment between what you believe and what you do when it would cost you something to act on it.

Humans were shaped by challenge, uncertainty, physical effort, and real-world consequences. These were not obstacles to our functioning, but the conditions of it. Remove them systematically, over years, and something essential erodes. Not all at once. By degrees. You become easier to distract, easier to placate, easier to compromise. And the worst of it is that it happens at a pace too gradual to name, so you never notice the moment you become a smaller version of yourself.

I noticed. Eventually. Several years into a high-functioning career that was, by every visible measure, succeeding, while something underneath it was very quietly failing.

Why Easy Is Not the Answer

The dominant response to this problem is more comfort. Wellness programs, mindfulness apps, four-day weeks, flexible working, optimized sleep. These are not worthless. But they treat the symptom. They add softness when what is needed, in many cases, is friction.

"Hard" has been mis-sold. We have come to associate it with punishment, with unnecessary suffering, with the macho cultural hangover of "no pain, no gain." That is not what I mean. I mean something precise: hardship that is chosen, structured, time-bounded, and oriented toward a purpose. Hardship with a finish line.

The difference between that and mere suffering is the difference between a Vision Quest and a grind. One builds you. One depletes you. The distinction is everything.

What This Book Will Do

This book makes one central argument: deliberate hardship, chosen and structured, restores what comfort erodes. Clarity. Self-respect. The capacity to act from your own values rather than from the path of least resistance.

It will show you why the voice that negotiates you downward, the one that arrives at mile 80 of a race, or at the moment a decision costs something, and begins its quiet work of reasonable-sounding retreat, is not wisdom. It is the product of a nervous system that has not been tested in a long time.

It will give you a framework. A modern Vision Quest, built on three bodies of evidence: the neuroscience of stress-induced growth, the anthropology of rites of passage across every human culture, and my own proof, of using structured hardship to recalibrate when the usual methods had stopped working.

And it will ask you to design your own ordeal. Not mine. Yours. Calibrated to where you are, what you have avoided, and what you need to prove to yourself.

> *You do not need to run 240 miles. You need to choose something that costs enough to matter, and finish it.*

How to Read This Book

The book is in four parts. They follow the same sequence as the transformation they describe.

Part I: The Problem. Names what is actually breaking in the modern leader and why. Ease, removal from nature, and the digital tsunami consuming executives and disembodying them from the teams they serve. It also makes the case that existing wellness solutions cannot fix a biological problem. Recovery is not the same as recalibration. Part I explains the difference.

Part II: The Ancient Solution. Before there were leadership consultants, there were vision quests. For millennia, societies used structured voluntary hardship to move adolescents into adulthood: strong, grateful, and prepared to contribute to something larger than themselves. Part II recovers what those traditions understood, explains the science of why the natural environment supports deep renewal, and introduces the concept of the Original Stack, the five-layer biological environment our hardware was actually designed for.

Part III: The Method. How to choose, design, and conduct your own modern vision quest. What the Descent requires, what it produces, and why the ordeal that costs enough to matter is the only kind that changes anything permanently.

Part IV: The Embodied Leader What you become when you return, and how to hold it. The Silverback in the boardroom. The 90-day return protocol. The three lintels of the Inner Citadel. Part IV is about converting the clarity earned in the wilderness into the way you lead in the room, every day, against the full force of the digital world trying to pull you back.

A Warning

After reading this book, you may decide that certain comforts you have been maintaining are not worth their cost. You may look at compromises you have made at work, in your thinking, in how you lead, and find that you can no longer make the case for them that you used to.

That is not a side effect. That is the point.

The comfort zone is not a safe place. It is a place where the slow erosion happens without your noticing. This book is an argument for leaving it. Not permanently, and not recklessly, but deliberately, on your own terms, for long enough to remember who you are when the noise stops.

You are more capable than your current conditions are asking you to be. That gap between what you are capable of and what you are being asked to do is not just a waste. Left unaddressed, it becomes damage.

Let's close it.

PART I - THE PROBLEM: WHY MODERN LEADERS ARE LOSING THEMSELVES

CHAPTER 1 - THE DAY I REALIZED LIFE HAD BECOME TOO EASY

Figure 1.1: Mile 205

The moment the argument stopped being theoretical. Thirty-five miles still to go, every rational case for stopping already made, and still moving.

The photograph above was taken at mile 205 of the Moab 240, a 240-mile footrace through the Utah desert. This is a portrait of a man who has finally stopped negotiating. I 'selfied' because something had landed in me with the force of a body punch. It didn't just ripple through my DNA; it rewrote it. I knew, standing in the dirt, that I needed to remember this exact feeling for the rest of my life.

I had just been through hell. I had endured sleep deprivation that blurred the line between reality and dreaming. I had navigated hallucinations, violent storms, profound isolation, and searing pain, running for three and a half days to that section. Yet, in the mountains, which felt like home at that point, I realized it hadn't broken me. On the contrary, I felt hardened. I was changed in every cell.

Moab 240 was my chosen vision quest in 2025. Standing there, with 35 miles still to go, I knew not only that I would finish, but that I was finally ready inside for what I had planned next.

But to understand why a 56-year-old man would voluntarily drag himself through 240 miles of desert purgatory, you have to understand the man I was ten months before that photo was taken.

Too Easy

December 2024. On paper, I was a man who had made it.

I work as a Venture Builder. My entire adult life has been dedicated to taking on difficult startup challenges and winning them. I built my first business in Coventry, England, worked in advertising agencies and media owners for a decade, built an outdoor advertising company on venture capital, moved to the US with the Wall Street Journal, fixed and sold the New York Institute of Finance, and eventually ran the US office of a major UK venture builder from the sun and comfort of Florida.

I was the person you called when the portfolio company was bleeding. "Hard things are fixed through hard work". I meant it. I lived by it.

But somewhere, without noticing, I had stopped being hard on myself.

I was accepting working practices that sandpapered my integrity. Not all at once, but a slow abrasion now and then. I disagreed with leadership approaches not because they were objectively wrong, but because they were wrong for the person I believed I was. Every morning I faced the same two options: speak up, cause the friction and risk the comfort, or stay quiet and keep the check. As time passed, I spoke up less, and I chose the check. I told myself this was collaborative. Sensible. Prudent.

I was living in high-functioning cognitive dissonance. And it was eating me from the inside.

The problem with shrinking is that it happens in increments too small to name. You don't step into a smaller room. You build it around yourself, wall by wall, each compromise so reasonable at the time that you don't notice the ceiling coming down. I wasn't failing. I was succeeding by every external measure while becoming a progressively diminished version of the person those successes were supposed to be for.

Where I once saw patterns and built strategy from them, I now heard noise. My judgment, the one thing I had always trusted, was blunted. Not broken. Blunted. And a blunted tool is more dangerous than a broken one, because you keep reaching for it.

The Invisible Ultra

> *Sidebar: An 'ultra-marathon' is anything over 50K and can go up to 500 miles, though 100 miles is the sweet spot. It's typically set in nature, in difficult but beautiful environments, mountains or deserts mostly. Running one takes 6–9 months of training, and completion rates average 60%. Beauty and pain, all wrapped up for you.*

Before we go further, I need to address something directly.

When I say my life had become "too easy," I mean the loss of productive friction, the seductive comfort of a life where nothing demands the full measure of you. That is one kind of problem.

But I know that for many of the leaders reading this, particularly those carrying the invisible weight of high-stakes careers alongside the domestic management that still falls disproportionately on women, that life does not feel easy. It feels relentless.

My daughter told me this when I described the book's premise. She said that for many people she knows, the idea of "seeking hardship" sounds elitist. Their daily existence is already an endurance sport. She was right to say it. And I needed to hear it.

I call this the Invisible Ultra. It is the unrelenting cognitive load of managing teams, raising children, holding domestic chaos together, and performing the emotional labor that makes everyone else's functioning possible. That is genuinely hard. Don't let anyone tell you otherwise.

But there is a critical distinction, one that this entire book rests on, between a Grind and a Quest.

The Invisible Ultra is a grind. It is unstructured, unending, and unappreciated pressure. It has no finish line. It does not build you. It depletes you, mile by mile, until there is nothing left to give and no sense of self separate from the giving.

A Vision Quest is the opposite. You are biologically wired for it. It is a hardship you choose, with a boundary around it, a purpose within it, and an endpoint you can see from the beginning. It does not add weight to your pack. It teaches you what you are actually carrying, and what you can set down.

We all need a finish line. Not because crossing it proves something to others. Because it proves something to you.

The Decision

There is a physical sensation to long-term cognitive dissonance that nobody warns you about. It is not dramatic. It does not announce itself. It is more like the quiet erosion of a riverbank, gradual, imperceptible, until one morning you step where solid ground used to be and find nothing. I had felt it for months before I could name it. I had been a sharp thinker. Decisive. Pattern-reading. And then, slowly, I wasn't.

You have to understand where I come from to understand what this cost me.

I was an amateur boxer. A street kid from a working-class neighborhood in Coventry, England. A place where you ordered your Christmas gifts from the local shoplifter and learned quickly to give no quarter or be walked over. Toughness was not a virtue there. It was infrastructure.

But I was a contradiction. I was a 'chav' (trailer trash is the US equivalent) who got out through books. I have been addicted to them my entire life. Mining them for ideas, methods, openings, edges. I read the way I boxed: looking for the angle, searching for the thing I could use. The Count of Monte Cristo. Mathematics. Whatever I could get my hands on.

On a Saturday morning run in December 2024, those two sides of me, the fighter and the reader, collided at exactly the right moment. I had been deep in the literature on vision quests and rites of passage. Ancient cultures. Structured hardship to reset identity. Something I had read before, but suddenly it landed differently. If entire civilizations had used deliberate ordeals to restore their people's power, to push them through the threshold, and bring them back changed, I could do the same. On my terms. In my time.

The goal was exact: toughen myself, reclaim my identity, restore the instrument.

I got back to my desk, sweat cooling, and signed up for the Moab 240.

I hit Submit. I smiled. And then, immediately: oh sh*t.

The weight of it arrived fast. Two hundred and forty miles

through the Utah desert. Four days. Brutal heat. Relentless elevation. I had raced shorter distances, 50 miles, 100 miles, and I was slow. I had missed timing cut-offs. I had failed and failed again. I struggled with the heat. I struggled with altitude.

So naturally, I had chosen a race defined by heat and altitude. A gauntlet thrown at myself. Prove to me that the chav from Coventry is still in there. Show me the kid who picked a fight on his first day of school and went home that evening to read.

The "oh sh*t" feeling is not a warning. It is a signal. It means the choice was real.

The Hard Fix

We have built a world of frictionless surfaces. We are never disconnected, never unstimulated, never asked to exert ourselves against anything that doesn't have an off switch. We tolerate, at work, things that contradict what we believe, because tolerance is the path of least resistance. It makes us smaller by degrees. Not weak. Diminished. There is a difference. Weaknesses can be addressed. A diminished person does not always know what has been lost.

Over-digitization, sustained cognitive dissonance, and repeated capitulation to the easier road had made a mess of my interior life. I needed a hard fix. Not a reframe. Not a retreat. A hard fix.

My vision quest took six months of preparation. The event itself was four days of sustained physical and mental brutality through the Utah desert. Many entrants did not finish. I did. Look at the photo at Mile 205. That is not the same person who hit Submit in December.

I am not asking you to run 240 miles. I am asking you to understand what deliberately chosen hardship did to me, and to consider what it might do for you. Not as punishment. Not as endurance tourism. As restoration.

But first, we need to change something more fundamental: how you think about the words “easy and hard", as everything that follows will require a different relationship with both.

And it should feel uncomfortable. That discomfort is information. It means you're still capable of being changed.

CHAPTER 2 - HARD VS EASY

At mile 191 on the Moab 240, it was pitch-black, raining sideways, and freezing. The storm, the fatigue, and the hallucinations had stripped everything away; there was no ambition left, no strategy, and no identity. My GPS watch was failing in the storm, and I realized I had been going the wrong way for an hour, sliding downhill in deep mud. I remember thinking that this must be what hell is like. You are moving forward, enduring searing pain, but you aren't getting anywhere.
Our business plans are our work GPS. We rely on them for cash planning, making hiring decisions, reporting to boards, and comparing ourselves to last year. A business can get hit with the mother of all storms, COVID being one example. Everyone had to find a new plan, no sitting around debating it, no chance to rethink, pivot, or die. Hard storms force clarity, bravery, and action.

I was miserable, and still had nine miles to go just to reach the next aid station. In that mud, I had to rely on mantras I had practiced for months just to take a single step. It was the hardest physical moment of my life. I tell you this not to impress you with the suffering. I tell you this because of what happened after, and because of what I noticed when I came home.

The contrast between that mountain and ordinary modern life is so extreme as to be almost absurd. And in that absurdity is something worth understanding.

The Hidden Tax

When you walk into an office building or a train station, you instinctively look for the escalator. You take it because it is easier, because you are in a hurry, or because you don't want to arrive at the meeting perspiring and out of breath. This is a reasonable decision by any immediate measure.

But most of modern life is engineered to produce exactly this calculation, dozens of times a day, across every domain: food, movement, conversation, and leadership—tools designed to remove effort at every turn. And while the escalator saves you energy today, it charges you something you won't notice until later.

The stairs are free training. Not free as in cheap, free as in already there, already paid for, requiring only the decision to use them. Stair climbing builds aerobic capacity, increases bone density, improves metabolic health, and reduces the risk of chronic disease. Large-scale studies published in the British Journal of Sports Medicine and the European Society of Cardiology found a 39% lower risk of dying from cardiovascular disease among regular stair climbers. You don't need a gym membership, a commute, or a schedule. You need only to stop looking for the escalator.

> *What appears harder in the moment is actually longer-term easier. What appears easier in the moment is actually longer-term harder. This asymmetry runs through every significant decision you will make.*

We face these micro-decisions dozens of times a day. To the uninitiated, the "easy" choice looks like a shortcut. To the initiated, it looks like a loan shark.

The easy choice charges you a high-interest rate on your future. The hard choice pays you compound interest. The maths always works the same way. Only the timeline changes.

The Tax in Practice

Consider managing a team. When an employee is underperforming, the easy choice is to fix their work yourself or to ignore it to avoid the awkwardness. It saves you ten minutes of discomfort today. The hidden tax is a team that cannot scale, and, eventually, your own burnout absorbs the load they were supposed to carry.

The hard choice is the direct conversation: clear standards, specific feedback, no softening. It costs you a difficult hour. It compounds into a high-performance culture. One hard hour now. Years of leverage later.

The same logic governs hiring. The easy choice is filling a gap with a mediocre candidate to end the search. The hard choice is leaving the seat empty until the right person appears. The mediocre hire taxes your time indefinitely, every week, requiring supervision that an A-player wouldn't need. The empty seat costs you nothing but patience.

This dynamic is no less corrosive in our living rooms. When feelings are hurt, the easy choice is the silent treatment, or "I'm fine," deployed to keep the peace. The tax is resentment that compounds quietly for years. The hard choice is the sentence that costs something: "What you said hurt me." It risks conflict at that moment. It purchases intimacy that silence never could.

With children, the easy choice is the iPad or sugar to stop the noise. It buys quiet now. It raises entitlement later. The hard choice is holding the boundary calmly while the noise continues. That is how resilience is built, in the child and in the parent. This one in particular feels so very easy to write, but incredibly hard to do as a parent in that moment, as the resistance is so high. They sit so quietly when you give them the iPad, you can finally get a break to get something done.

These decisions come at you across twenty to thirty choice points every day, across food, work, movement, and love. The accumulated weight of them, made without awareness, is what turns capable people into diminished versions of themselves. You are not fighting a lack of discipline.

You are fighting your own biology.

The Biology of Easy

Your brain is running software designed for the Serengeti, not for a world of safe cities, sugar in every shop, and warm rooms with infinite entertainment. It prioritizes immediate reward because, to your ancestors, tomorrow was genuinely not promised. This is Hyperbolic Discounting: the biological mandate to take the small, immediate reward now over the larger, less visible one later. It kept your ancestors alive. In the modern world, it is slowly making you smaller.

Simultaneously, your body is a miser. It is obsessed with fuel efficiency. The Law of Least Effort, physically routing neural pathways toward the path of least resistance to conserve glucose. In the wild, this efficiency kept you alive. In a world where survival requires almost no physical effort, it locks you into a loop of progressive lethargy.

These are not character flaws. They are design features of a system built for a world of outdoor hardship that no longer exists. Understanding this matters so you override a system operating in constant comfort it wasn't designed for. The mechanism is Hormesis.

Hormesis is the biological reality that short, controlled bursts of stress do not degrade the system. They upgrade it. The shock of cold water, the strain of a heavy lift, the sustained focus of deep work, these stress triggers a cellular response that rebuilds the organism stronger than it was before. Not despite the discomfort. Because of it.

> *Hard isn't the enemy. Hard is the system upgrade.*

Rewiring Hard

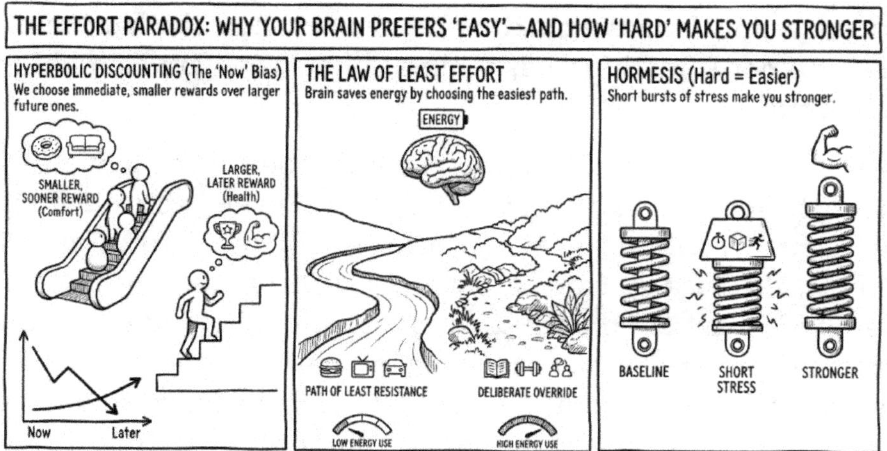

Figure 2.1: The Effort Paradox

The less you demand of yourself, the harder everything becomes. This framework shows the mechanism by which comfort compounds into incapacity.

We have to stop treating the word "hard" as a warning label. It is a prompt.

When you look at a task, a ten-mile climb, a difficult firing, a conversation you have been avoiding for three weeks, and you label it "hard," you are doing more than describing difficulty. You are issuing instructions to your nervous system. You are typing a command that reads: threat detected, prepare for damage. Your brain, obedient as ever, responds by flooding your bloodstream with cortisol. Heart rate spikes. Vision tunnels. Higher-order thinking clouds. You have primed yourself for struggle before you have taken the first step.

You have turned a hill into a wall.

Elite athletes do not process "hard" as a threat. They process it as a signal. When the pain arrives, they don't recoil, they recognize it. They know that the sensation of difficulty is the physical feeling of capacity expanding. Courtney Dauwalter, a professional ultra-runner, with the most relentlessly cheerful disposition, calls it the 'pain cave'. She knows real hardship will manifest. It appears in every race. She imagines herself chipping away at its walls with a pickaxe, mile by mile, making the cave smaller. The hard miles then, are not something happening to her. They are something she is doing.

I learned a version of this on the step climber in the gym, long before the mountains of Utah. When I hit a steep incline and my mind starts to whimper, or my legs start to burn, I force myself to smile. Not because I am happy. Because it confuses the system. The physical act of smiling sends a signal back along the vagus nerve: we are safe, we are hunting, not being hunted. It shifts the nervous system from a threat state to a challenge state. The same stimulus, processed differently, produces a different result entirely.

Bring this same disposition into the business.

In the companies I help lead, I have introduced a single question into meetings: "What is interesting and hard right now that we should be handling?" Notice the shift. By pairing "hard" with "interesting," the problem stops being a burden and starts being a puzzle. Curiosity replaces anxiety. The team moves toward the problems with the outsized payoffs rather than retreating into the busywork that carries no risk.

This is replicable. It is a practice, not a personality type.

The Choice

The next time you feel that resistance, the pull toward the escalator, the postponed call, the skipped workout, the thing you have been meaning to say, recognize it for what it is.

It is not a stop sign. It is a junction.

The universe is asking whether you want to pay the tax or earn the interest. It asks this question every day, in dozens of small moments, and in a handful of large ones. The answer you give shapes, incrementally and then irreversibly, the person you become.

Stop waiting for it to feel easy. **Choose hard.**

Figure 2.2: The Easy-Hard Elevator
You are always moving in one direction or the other. There is no static floor.

Further Resources & References

Moab 240 Runners manual: https://docs.google.com/document/d/1FfDF55gYQJ4J36rxxnLlBCTd4Kv0TGvH6u8_l46elwE/
Pole Canyon (mi 185.51) to Geyser Pass (mi 200.51)

Framing Effects (Kahneman & Tversky): The original research on how different phrasing changes decision-making and emotional response. ***The seminal paper (PDF):*** *Tversky, A., & Kahneman, D. (1981). Science, 211(4481), 453-458.* ***A more accessible overview:*** *The Decision Lab: Why does the way information is presented affect our decisions?*

Self-Efficacy (Albert Bandura): Research on how our belief in our abilities affects how we approach difficult tasks (viewing them as threats vs. challenges). ***Overview by Bandura (PDF):*** *Bandura, A. (1994). Self-efficacy. In V. S. Ramachaudran (Ed.), Encyclopedia of human behavior (Vol. 4, pp. 71-81). New York: Academic Press.* ***The American Psychological Association summary:*** *Teaching tip sheet: Self-efficacy.*

Cognitive Appraisal Theory (Lazarus & Folkman): This theory explains the mechanism by which a stressor is instantly categorized as either a "threat" or a "challenge." ***A good academic summary of the theory:*** *ScienceDirect Topics: Cognitive Appraisal* ***Related study on threat vs. challenge states:*** *Blascovich, J., & Mendes, W. B. (2000). Challenge and threat appraisals. (ResearchGate link to book chapter)*

Smiling Uphill Technique on Gym Climber: Book: How Bad do you Want it by Matt Fitzgerald

Climb Stairs to Live Longer Study: https://www.escardio.org/news/press/press-releases/Climb-stairs-to-live-longer/

The Hard vs. Easy Cheat Sheet

Figure 2.3: Hard vs. Easy: The Cheat Sheet

The decision matrix that determines whether to make life better or worse.

The Scenario	The "Easy" Choice (The Loan)	The "Hard" Choice (The Investment)	The Payoff
Management	Fixing the work yourself.	Radical Candor conversations.	A scalable team.
Hiring	Hiring the "Okay" candidate.	Leaving the seat empty for the A-Player.	Leverage & Performance.
Love	The "Silent Treatment."	Vulnerability ("That hurt me").	Intimacy & Trust.
Finance	Lifestyle Creep (New car).	Banking the difference.	Freedom (The ability to quit).
Anxiety	Doomscrolling social media.	Sitting in Silence.	Mental Clarity.
Team Morale/ Family Crisis	"Everything is fine" (Protective Shielding)	This is falling apart, and here is how we fix it. (Truth Telling)	Trust and Shared Load*

**Women often burn out because they don't share the load; the "Hard" choice is admitting they need the team/family to step up.*

CHAPTER 3 - THE EXECUTIVE NERVOUS SYSTEM CRISIS

As I write this, my desk is less a workspace than a command center for a losing battle.

Four company email addresses. Teams, WhatsApp, LinkedIn, Slack, iMessage, all firing. A calendar of back-to-back meetings that ricochets from a performance issue, to a board report, to a client strategy session, each one demanding a different version of me at full capacity. By hour eight of a twelve-hour day, I am spent. And underneath the exhaustion is something worse: the sinking, specific feeling that I haven't done any real work.

I have processed noise. I have not found the signal.

This feeling has a name. Leaders across industries recognize it instantly when they hear it, and almost none of them talk about it openly.

Busy but Hollow

It is the specific malaise of the modern executive, not the exhaustion of effort, but the exhaustion of fragmentation—the particular despair of having been productive all day at the wrong level. You have cleared the inbox, attended the calls, and responded to the pings. The dashboard looks active. But you know, in the way that the body knows things before the mind admits them, that you haven't moved the actual dial. You have been mistaking velocity for direction. And the two are not the same thing.

> *We are doing more than ever and achieving less depth. The problem isn't pace. It's the fact that the pace is being applied in the wrong direction.*

The disruption of AI has compounded this. A technology with more sweeping societal impact than the internet has simultaneously destroyed many companies' defensive moats, democratized innovation, and dropped the barrier to entry for new digital products to near zero. The competitive noise has compounded. The pressure to adapt has intensified. The window for deep thought has narrowed further still.

How many times are you on your phone in a meeting right now? Be honest. How often is your time fractured between two obligations simultaneously, or three? Add the hours scrolled on social media, the notifications processed, the micro-decisions made. How can you possibly lead others with this behavior? We were not designed for this. The evidence is accumulating that the environment is not merely inconvenient. It is physiologically hostile.

Contrast this to another type of leader, an embodied leader in the wild.

The Silverback Gorilla. In nature, he does five specific things:

He regulates, he doesn't react. When a threat arrives, the silverback becomes still before he moves. That stillness is information: the group watches him to calibrate. If he charges, they know it's real. If he doesn't move, they settle. His nervous system sets the floor for the group's.

He absorbs the external threat, so the group doesn't have to. Predators, rival males, encroaching territory: all of that is his problem. The rest of the group gets to focus on eating, raising young, and building social bonds. He takes the friction so they can do the work.

He leads by presence, not instruction. There is no delegation, no town hall, no performance review. The group orients around him spatially. Where he goes, they go. His conviction is demonstrated, not announced.

He enforces the boundary once, clearly. He doesn't escalate gradually, give warnings, or manage the situation. When a line is crossed, he responds with full force, once, and then it's over. No grudge, no drawn-out conflict, no performance. Decisive, then done.

He is most visible when things are hardest. When food is scarce, he eats last. When the path is dangerous, he goes first. The group's sense of safety is directly proportional to his willingness to be at the front of the difficult thing.

Do not confuse this embodied leadership with a masculine-only trait. A single matriarch leads the Savanna Elephant herd. The oldest, biggest female. She also decides how the herd behaves, with leadership based on wisdom and memory, not just physicality. Though she has that in abundance.

It's impossible to be an embodied leader from the neck up.

The Anatomy of Fracture

Technology shifts the focus from felt presence to informational exchange. To understand why this feels so terrible, and why it is making us weaker leaders, we have to look at the biology. We are running software designed for the natural world on hardware plugged into a global, infinite digital matrix.

The part of your brain responsible for moving the dial on strategy, complex decision-making, empathy, and long-term planning is the Prefrontal Cortex (PFC). It is the CEO of your brain, and it has a fatal flaw: it is the most energy-expensive organ in the body and the first to fail under sustained cognitive load.

Every time you switch from a strategy document to an email, your brain is forced to context-switch. The American Psychological Association has found that shifting between tasks can cost up to 40% of productive time. Apply that to your own week. For me, even with deliberate effort to batch and protect my time, it feels like a 20% tax at minimum.

But the more devastating number is this: it takes an average of 23 minutes and 15 seconds to return to deep focus after a single interruption. If you check your phone every ten minutes, which the data suggests most executives do, you are biologically incapable of deep thought. Not less capable. Incapable. You are permanently operating in the shallows.

> *If you are interrupted more frequently than you can recover from, you are not doing knowledge work. You are performing the appearance of it.*

The Dopamine Trap

Why do we do this to ourselves? Why do I check the fourth email inbox when I know the strategy document is sitting there, more important, and half-finished?

Because the real work is hard, it requires sustained effort with no immediate reward. Checking an email, clearing a notification, and firing off a Slack reply each provide a micro-dose of dopamine. It feels like productivity. It satisfies the brain's completion bias. We are, in the most clinical sense, feeding an addiction: snacking on the empty calories of information, spiking the reward circuit, while starving ourselves of the protein of deep work that generates actual satisfaction.

This is why we feel hollow. Not lazy. Not undisciplined. Chemically diverted. The system has been hacked by a thousand product designers whose entire job is to make sure you never stop checking.

It gets worse. The damage runs deeper than productivity. It is physical.

Every notification, the ping from Teams, the vibration in your pocket, the red badge on an app, is processed by your brain as a micro-threat. It triggers the orienting reflex. Your body activates something called the HPA Axis: the Hypothalamic-Pituitary-Adrenal cascade. This helps you survive a predator. Cortisol and adrenaline flood the bloodstream to get you ready to rumble!

In the acute, short-term context for which the HPA Axis evolved, it is lifesaving. In the chronic state of the modern executive, where we touch our phones an average of 2,617 times per day, we are then bathing our nervous system in a corrosive, continuous drip of stress hormones that it was never designed to sustain.

The effects are not uniform. Men under chronic cortisol load tend to detach. They become transactional, avoidant, or short-fused. Women under the same load tend to over-function: the "tend and befriend" stress response drives them to absorb more, manage more, smooth more, until the autoimmune system, the body's last line of complaint, begins to fail. Different presentations, same underlying damage.

The cost to leadership is measurable. A University of London study found that constant digital interruptions reduce an executive's effective IQ by 10 points, more than double the cognitive impact of smoking marijuana. We are, quite literally, leading our organizations while cognitively impaired by distraction.

So we are now putting off the real work, and we're dumber. But what may be even worse is that empathy is the next casualty. A calm Prefrontal Cortex and active mirror neurons are the biological prerequisites for genuine connection with other people.

When cortisol levels are elevated, the brain shifts into survival mode. In survival mode, your team stops appearing to you as humans to be led and begins appearing as obstacles to be managed or threats to be neutralized. You become transactional. Your people sense it. They always do, and so the stress propagates outward through the organization like a current.

Willpower compounds all of this. It is a finite daily resource. By 2:00 PM, after 200 emails and 40 micro-decisions, the decision tank is empty. What follows is not bad judgment. It is the absence of judgment: decisions deferred until tomorrow or made on impulse to end the cognitive pain.

The Red Queen Effect

Layered over all of this is a specific modern anxiety that has no historical precedent.

In Lewis Carroll's Through the Looking-Glass, the Red Queen tells Alice: "Now, here, you see, it takes all the running you can do, to keep in the same place." Evolutionary biologists borrowed the concept. So has the modern workplace.

AI has increased the metabolic rate of business. The half-life of a professional skill, that is, the period before it becomes obsolete, was estimated at roughly 30 years a generation ago. Current estimates put it at five years and shrinking fast. This is not merely a career management problem. It is a source of existential anxiety that runs beneath every leadership decision: the terror that if you stop spinning the plates for one second, you will become irrelevant.

So we add more apps. Join more channels. Attempt to drink from the firehose. The response to information overload is, paradoxically, more information. And the spiral tightens. If the speed of change continues to quicken, which it will, at what point will your biological hardware fail? For many, it's already happened. We are seeing a huge trend for 'Slow Living' and nature recalibration. But for leaders who must plug into the digital highway to grow their organizations, there is no such escape. What are we supposed to do?

The Broken Compass

We have to stop blaming ourselves for a lack of discipline and recognize the truth: we are operating in a deliberately hostile environment. The environment is engineered to consume our attention. Individually, we cannot out-willpower it. We need a protocol. We need to treat attention as the scarce resource it is. As vital, as finite, and as worth protecting, as precious as the clean water I carried in my pack across the Utah desert.

In the last two months of training for the Moab 240, I had a Plantar fasciitis injury; the physical pain was often excruciating, but it was too late to reduce my training load. However, the mental task of dealing with it was mercifully simple: put one foot in front of the other, drink, eat, repeat, ignore. I found running on the edge of my foot helped reduce it, plus CBD and Ibuprofen. In the Moab 240 race, it was debilitatingly painful on day one, disappeared completely on days two and three, and returned on day four. No idea why. Despite the pain, the objective was clear. Progress was visible. Every step was either toward the finish or away from it.

Contrast that physical suffering to straightforward mental tasks in the office. Cognitive overload is accelerating for knowledge workers, but the physical requirements are near zero. We sit in ergonomic chairs and move between climate-controlled rooms. Coffee from machines that do the hard grinding is kindly brought to us during our back-to-back meetings, so we don't even have to stand up. Movement and physical exertion removed. Is it pain-free? I know you know the answer is no. Mental environment is invisible, complex, and structurally hostile. We are digitally overloaded, chemically hijacked, and cognitively fractured. We are busy. But we are lost.

Give me the Plantar fasciitis pain I can clearly feel anytime vs the slow poison from knowledge work, that invisibly dismantles your wellbeing from within.

For years, before I could name it, I carried a specific sense that my mind-only work, the knowledge-worker existence, with its spreadsheets and strategies and screens, was leaving me operating at a fraction of what I was capable of. That somewhere in the separation of mind from body, I had unplugged something essential. And it is causing an unknown decay in my functioning, I couldn't name. It is one of the reasons I started the business Root Astro. It feels wrong that we spend so much time with mind and body working separately.

Neuroscience has confirmed the instinct. The brain is not a self-contained processor. It is a hungry organ that depends on the body's metabolic and sensory activity to function at capacity. The discovery of the Somato-Cognitive Action Network (SCAN) reveals the executive control centers in the brain. The structures responsible for planning, complex reasoning, and high-level decision-making are physically hardwired into our motor circuits. Sedentary "thinking work" does not merely leave the body underused. It effectively unplugs the ignition to our own intelligence.

I spent years in boardrooms as a head in a jar: navigating abstract data and strategic documents while my physical self sat separate from the task at hand, dormant. I was not just getting soft. I was operating in low-power mode without knowing it.

We need to disconnect to reconnect. We need to choose hard.

Voluntary hardship is not masochism. It is a recalibration. When we step out of the ergonomic chair and into the physical grit of a vision quest, the brain stops ruminating on abstract anxieties. It begins solving the immediate, concrete problems of the physical world: gravity, fatigue, terrain. It releases Brain-Derived Neurotrophic Factor (BDNF), the Miracle-Gro of neuroplasticity. This rebuilds the neural connections that the digital environment has been slowly severing. The motor cortex re-links to the executive mind. The fog lifts. What emerges is not merely relief from stress. It is a different quality of thought entirely.

> *We find that the only way to truly think with everything we are is to finally start doing with everything we have.*

Chapter Tool: Is Your Executive Nervous System in Crisis?

This is a three-step tool. 1. Read each statement and check the ones that apply to your current professional life. Be honest, this is diagnostic, not evaluative. Step 2: Count your score—step 3. Review the table showing what good and bad look like, and place yourself to the left or right in each row.

Phase 1. Digital Overload & Sensory Saturation

Figure 3.1: Is Your Executive Nervous System in Crisis?
The diagnostic. Four phases, each more costly than the last, and most leaders are already past phase one before they start looking.

Statement	Check
My first act of the day (within 15 minutes of waking) is checking email or messaging apps.	☐
I feel a reflexive urge to check my phone even when it hasn't pinged.	☐
I rarely spend more than 20 minutes on a single task without an interruption.	☐
I find it physically difficult to read a long document without my attention fragmenting.	☐

Phase 2. Decision Fatigue & Cognitive Rust

Statement	Check

By 4:00 PM, I defer important decisions because I lack the mental energy to weigh them.	☐
I frequently second-guess decisions made under pressure.	☐
Late in the day, I default to the easiest path rather than the most strategic one.	☐
My irritability with colleagues increases significantly in the final two hours of the workday.	☐

Phase 3. The Busy but Hollow Metric

Statement	Check
I often finish a ten-hour day unable to name a single meaningful contribution I made.	☐
My calendar is back-to-back, with zero white space for reflection or deep work.	☐
I perform high-speed administrative work to avoid the weight of complex, strategic work.	☐
I feel a growing gap between my values and how I actually spend my hours.	☐

Phase 4. The Mind-Body Break

Statement	Check
I treat my body primarily as a vehicle to carry my head from meeting to meeting.	☐
I spend more than eight hours a day sitting and being sedentary.	☐
I rarely solve problems with my hands or engage in high-effort physical movement.	☐
I experience brain fog that caffeine does not clear.	☐

Now, total up your checks from above and find your range below:

Range	
0–4	**The Resilient Leader** You have maintained strong boundaries and protected your biological hardware. You are likely operating with high fluid intelligence and real strategic bandwidth.
5–9	**The Fragile Executive** Yellow Zone. Your nervous system is beginning to prioritize short-term survival over long-term strategy. The fracture is early and reversible. This is the right time to act.
10+	**System Shutdown** You are experiencing a full-scale Executive Nervous System Crisis. Your effective IQ is suppressed, your empathy is eroding, and your decision-making is compromised by chronic cortisol exposure. The rest of this book is for you.

Now review your score and consider what good and bad look like below, and which column you feel you mostly live in on each row:

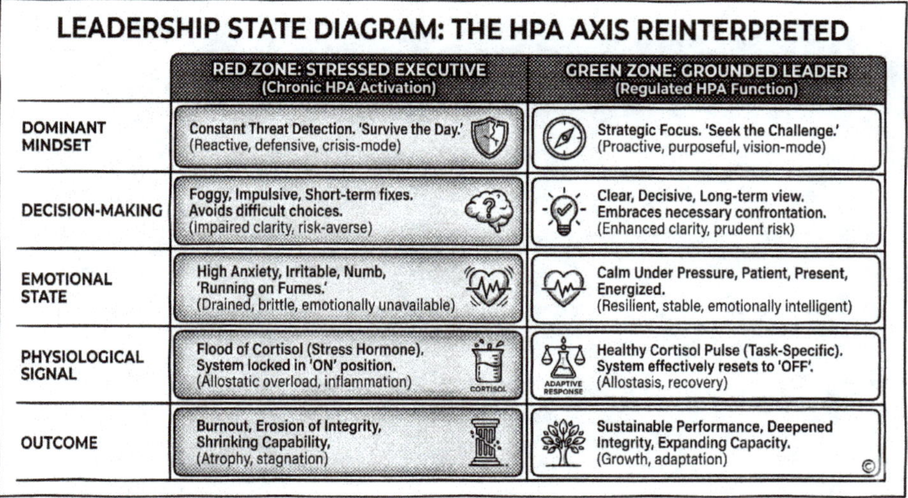

LEADERSHIP STATE DIAGRAM: THE HPA AXIS REINTERPRETED

	RED ZONE: STRESSED EXECUTIVE (Chronic HPA Activation)	GREEN ZONE: GROUNDED LEADER (Regulated HPA Function)
DOMINANT MINDSET	Constant Threat Detection. 'Survive the Day.' (Reactive, defensive, crisis-mode)	Strategic Focus. 'Seek the Challenge.' (Proactive, purposeful, vision-mode)
DECISION-MAKING	Foggy, Impulsive, Short-term fixes. Avoids difficult choices. (Impaired clarity, risk-averse)	Clear, Decisive, Long-term view. Embraces necessary confrontation. (Enhanced clarity, prudent risk)
EMOTIONAL STATE	High Anxiety, Irritable, Numb, 'Running on Fumes.' (Drained, brittle, emotionally unavailable)	Calm Under Pressure, Patient, Present, Energized. (Resilient, stable, emotionally intelligent)
PHYSIOLOGICAL SIGNAL	Flood of Cortisol (Stress Hormone). System locked in 'ON' position. (Allostatic overload, inflammation)	Healthy Cortisol Pulse (Task-Specific). System effectively resets to 'OFF'. (Allostasis, recovery)
OUTCOME	Burnout, Erosion of Integrity, Shrinking Capability. (Atrophy, stagnation)	Sustainable Performance, Deepened Integrity, Expanding Capacity. (Growth, adaptation)

Figure 3.2: The Leadership State Diagram

Where you are operating from determines what decisions you are capable of making. This maps the terrain.

Further Resources & References

Context switching cost: American Psychological Association, shifting between tasks costs up to 40% of productive time.

Recovery time: University of California, Irvine : average 23 minutes 15 seconds to return to deep focus after interruption.

Phone touches: Dscout (2016) : average 2,617 touches per day.

IQ impact: University of London : constant digital interruptions reduce effective IQ by 10 points (vs 5 points for marijuana).

Empathy erosion: Scientific Reports (2023): high cognitive load reduces mirror neuron engagement.

AI burnout: Quantum Workplace (2024) frequent AI users report 45% higher burnout rates.

CEO mental health: 55% of CEOs reported a major mental health issue in the past year (2024), a 24-point increase.

SCAN: Somato-Cognitive Action Network, discovery linking motor circuits to executive control centers.

BDNF: Brain-Derived Neurotrophic Factor, released during physical exertion; supports neuroplasticity and synaptic repair.

CHAPTER 4 - WHY WELLNESS AND COMFORT ALONE FAIL

You cannot meditate your way out of a crisis of character. There are many solutions to the crisis I describe in Chapter 3. The Global Wellness Economy is valued at $5.6 trillion. We have never spent more money on feeling better. And anxiety is at record highs. If the solution to the executive nervous system crisis were a meditation app or a corporate wellness retreat, we would all be enlightened by now.

These tools are not worthless. Deep rest is a biological requirement. Meditation, forest bathing, and recovery protocols are essential for what I call Phase 1 work—reducing cortisol, processing emotion, restoring baseline capacity. Retreats clear the mind of the onslaught of messaging and escaping the hostile environment, so you can catch your breath at least!

But it's not enough. The operating system is compromised, fragmented, identity-eroded, and structurally weakened. It has not had the chance to put its natural capabilities to the test and develop the resilience, self-confidence & calm that comes from operating as designed. Both mind and body together.

I was an amateur boxer. Boxers that don't 'spar' with strong fighters in training typically lose their matches, in my experience. They are not fight-ready. Their mind and body have not operated at the level needed to win. I trained with Richard Evatt, an outstanding puncher who went on to be the IBO featherweight champion as a professional. He hit you with a god-like power and is considered by many to be the hardest-hitting pound-for-pound fighter to come out of the UK. I never lost a fight while he was my sparring partner. Everyone I boxed was a relative walk in the park after suffering him in training.

> *Recovery and recalibration are not the same thing. We don't just need to recover from our lives. We need to recalibrate the machines that live them.*

The Wellness Industry's Fundamental Error

Remember the Hormesis from Chapter 2? This biological pillar that controls stress, applied intentionally, does not degrade your system; it upgrades it. Muscles rebuild stronger after they tear. Immune systems strengthen after exposure. The stressor is not the problem. The stressor is the mechanism.

The wellness industry's fundamental error is not adding the stressor.

We have already excelled at this in our 'civilized' world: temperature-controlled rooms, food delivered to the door, conflict-avoidant HR policies, ergonomic everything. We have systematically eliminated the hormetic friction that kept our nervous systems calibrated—an over-stimulated executive arriving at a 5-star retreat, pampered and calmed for that weekend. But returned to the frontline softer than arrival. They haven't developed the callus needed to withstand friction. They've just applied lotion.

The spa is not the enemy. It just doesn't finish the job. We are swords that have gone blunt. We don't need a velvet pillow alone.

We need sharpening. In martial arts, fighters are often referred to as 'looking sharp'. Meaning their mind and body are dialed into the task at hand. Confident, capable, resilient, 100% present. Fight-ready.

The Real Disease: Cognitive Dissonance

What modern leaders are suffering from is not a lack of relaxation. It is a lack of confrontation.

No amount of lavender oil closes that gap. The only way to close it is to stare it in the face.

In the Moab 240, I could not mindfulness my way back up a mountain at 3 AM after going the wrong way, vertically down, sliding in deep mud, and falling painfully on rocks for over an hour. I could not hack the thirty-degree rain. I had to confront my own weakness, the despair, the physical limitations, and watch people better adapted to altitude move speedily past me in the dark. That confrontation is where the growth happened. Not in the recovery tent. On the climb.

Leaders today are treated like fragile vases that need protection. In reality, we are a bag of water and bones with a prefrontal cortex, standing in fluorescent light, checking a screen. The problem is not the pressure. The problem is that we have forgotten what we are made of.

I have been there. I have a meditation app and meditate daily. Those ten minutes of guided calm are not enough to counterbalance twelve hours of chaotic, reactive leadership. (It gets me to mid-morning!) The reason it doesn't is not a failure of willpower or consistency. It is a failure to understand how identity is formed. Rich Roll, a podcaster and recovering alcoholic, states that "mood follows action". I think that's because identity does too.

Behavioral psychology explains this with its 'Self-Perception Theory'. Identity is not formed by what we think, or what we listen to, or what we intend. It is formed by evidence. Specifically, by the evidence our own behavior produces about who we are. We watch ourselves act, and we draw conclusions about our identity. Our brains synthesize between action and intent, and updates.

The implications are merciless:

If you sit in a meeting and hold your tongue when you should speak, you teach yourself: I am a coward.

If you check your phone when you promised your child you would play, you teach yourself: I am distracted.

We know we should be strategic. But following thousands of phone touches, we are reactive.

Modern wellness alone is too passive. It doesn't ask enough of you. You cannot build a stronger identity through an experience that requires nothing.

The Missing Ingredient: Ordeal

Anthropology gives us the answer the wellness industry hasn't reached.

For thousands of years, across every culture, the Spartan Agoge, the Indigenous American Vision Quest, the Aboriginal Walkabout, and the Stoic voluntary discomfort practices, human beings understood something we have collectively forgotten: to move from one stage of life to a higher one, you needed an Ordeal.

Not a spa. Not a retreat. An Ordeal: a structured, voluntary challenge that pushes you to your limit and forces a system reboot. The Ordeal is not a metaphor. It is a mechanism.

> *You cannot consume your way to strength. You have to earn it through a different kind of movement.*

Deep change requires neuroplasticity. The brain's ability to rewire itself. Neuroplasticity is triggered by two conditions: focus and urgency, driven neurochemically by acetylcholine and norepinephrine. You do not find urgency in a hammock. It appears when you are at mile 200 of a race, or running low on water, or confronting a fear you have carried for years. The Ordeal floods the system with the neurochemistry that genuine change requires. It demands total presence. You cannot check your email in an ice bath. You cannot fake it on a mountain.

The reason wellness falls short is that it asks nothing of you. An Ordeal asks everything. And because it asks everything, it returns something that comfort never can.

Self-respect.

> *The wellness industry has offered us painkillers. We need surgery. Not to suffer, but to set the bone properly, so the healing is real.*

Both Are Required

To be clear: this is not an argument against rest. Rest is a biological necessity. Meditation, recovery, sleep, nature, journaling, these are important tools. My partner at Root Astro is an executive coach for CEOs and educates on Strategic Rest as part of her overall methodology. This rest is Phase 1: the space in which the body repairs, the mind processes, and the nervous system returns to baseline.

But Phase 1 without Phase 2 is hiding. You are restoring your capacity, only to return it to the same conditions that depleted it. The recovery becomes a loop rather than a ladder.

Phase 2. The Ordeal, the voluntary confrontation, the structured hard thing, is what transforms the recovered person into a recalibrated one. It builds the evidence that changes the identity. It earns the self-respect that no app can provide.

The soft provides the space to reflect. The hard provides the strength to act on those reflections. Without the hard, the soft becomes escapism. Without the soft, the hard is just punishment.

We have diagnosed the disease: a life stripped of friction is stripping us of our humanity. In Part II, we stop looking at the problem. We turn to the solution. This is the ancient pattern used by the Greeks, the Lakota, and the Stoics. They didn't have Zoom. But they knew how to build unshakeable leaders.

It is time to see what they knew that we have forgotten.

Chapter Tool: The Recalibration Ledger

Use this as a reference when deciding which mode you need. The answer is almost always both, in sequence.

Phase	Label	Best For
Phase 1	Recovery (The Still)	Reducing immediate cortisol. Processing emotions. Mental rest. Restoring baseline capacity.
Phase 2	Recalibration (The Hard)	Expanding your window of tolerance. Resetting identity through evidence. Building the callus that holds under pressure.
The Goal	*Don't use recovery to hide from your life. Use it to prepare for the next hard thing.*	

PART II - THE ANCIENT SOLUTION: HOW HUMANS USED TO FIND CLARITY

CHAPTER 5 - VISION QUESTS: WHAT THEY ARE AND WHAT YOU GET

I often looked at my mother with surprise, wonder, and something close to astonishment.

A small woman, thin, barely five-foot-three, but fiery and courageous beyond her size. She would square up to my father, an ex-professional boxer, with whatever kitchen equipment was at hand, depending on his latest transgression. In The New Star, our family pub in Coventry, the rowdiest patrons weren't afraid of the heavyweight behind the bar. They were terrified of the pocket rocket patrolling the floor.

Figure 5.1: Post-Fight, 1972
My father, my mother, my sister, and I after his first British Title fight. The lesson: looking tough and being tough are different things.

Her presence wasn't a bluff. It was a biological reality. She was the angel to those who needed her, and she was the fire to those who threatened the peace. She could be both, completely, because she wasn't afraid of either. She occupied a space that was already won, because she had built a fortress within: one where her character was the only currency that mattered.

Years later, when I began reading about resilience and came across the Stoic concept of the Inner Citadel, the image that immediately came to mind was not of Marcus Aurelius. It was my mother standing in that Coventry pub. The Inner Citadel, as Aurelius used it, describes a spiritual fortress within the mind: a place of absolute inner authority that no external adversity can reach. My mother hadn't read the Stoics. She had lived them.

> *Leadership is the art of maintaining your Inner Citadel so that you can be the fire when justice demands it, and the angel when your people need it.*

Most modern leaders are porous. Every email, every market dip, every snarky comment leaks into their system and poisons their judgment. They lead from the amygdala, in a state of chronic fight-or-flight. But a leader who has built their Inner Citadel leads with what appears an unfazed smile: the calm at the center of the storm that comes not from the absence of pressure, but from having banked enough stress to know that the daily friction of business barely registers.

The Stoics believed the Citadel was built through philosophy, reflection, and being at one with nature. My experience in the boardroom and on the trail taught me something they didn't publish: you cannot build a stone fortress on a foundation of sand. To truly own your Inner Citadel, you have to upgrade the biology beneath it.

The Source Code Rewrite

For thousands of years, humans have intuitively understood something that modern biology is only now able to measure: if you want to change the spirit, you must first challenge the body.

The Lakota and Anishinaabe people are Indigenous Americans with roots in the Great Lakes, deeply and spiritually connected to the land. They remain in the US today, fierce protectors of their sovereignty and recognized as domestic dependent nations. They practiced the Hanbleceya, "crying for a vision." A young man is sent into the wilderness for four days without food or water, isolated on a mountain ledge or in a pit. The goal is to strip away the comforts of the village and force a confrontation with the self. We have tended to view these rites as purely spiritual. But what they are engineering, without the language for it, is epigenetic change.

Think of your DNA not as a fixed stone tablet, but as a vast library of instruction manuals. In a comfortable modern life, most of those manuals are sealed shut. Your body never needs them, so it never opens them. A 240-mile journey through sleep deprivation, hallucination, and physical breakdown is a cellular emergency signal. It informs the system that the standard operating procedures used to run a board meeting or manage a portfolio are insufficient for the demands now being made.

So the body initiates DNA methylation. It chemically tags specific genes and forces open those sealed manuals. Studies on ultra-endurance athletes show that after extreme exertion, the body rapidly alters the genes governing inflammation, metabolic efficiency, and cellular repair. You are forcing access to a survival mode that a sedentary life will never unlock. And crucially, once those genes are switched on, they do not immediately switch off. You return to your daily life running on an upgraded operating system.

The Biological Inner Citadel

While the cells are updating their software, the brain is upgrading its hardware.

There is a specific moment in every vision quest. The reasons you started, dissolve. For me it arrived at mile 140 of the Moab, day three. The ego goes quiet. All that remains is a raw, pressurised desire to stop. Neuroscience has located precisely where that battle takes place.

It is a small structure called the Anterior Midcingulate Cortex (aMCC). Dr. Andrew Huberman describes this region "as the seat of the will to live". More precisely: it is the physical location in the brain of doing what you do not want to do. In people who consistently choose the path of least resistance, this structure atrophies. In the leader who takes the difficult call, manages the underperforming colleague, runs the extra mile, it thickens.

You are physically growing the hardware required for tenacity.

The aMCC has neuroplasticity. Every time you move toward friction when everything in you wants to move away, you are performing high-repetition strength training for this specific structure. Post-mortem and MRI scans of SuperAgers, people in their eighties with the cognitive sharpness of twenty-five-year-olds, consistently show a thick, robust aMCC. This is why the eighty-year-old chairman often has more fight in him than the thirty-year-old associate: not wisdom, not experience, but decades of deliberate friction. Heavy-repetition weightlifting for the will, while the culture around them trained people to seek comfort.

When you say you are hard-headed, you are not speaking in metaphor. You have built a physical infrastructure of tenacity that outlasts the race.

Hormesis and the Noise Floor

There is a paradox at the center of stress. Chronic, low-grade stress, the kind produced by a difficult boss, a fractured inbox, or daily ambient anxiety, shortens lifespan. This kind of stress accelerates deterioration. It literally wears the body down biologically.

But acute, voluntary, massive stress does the opposite. This is hormesis: a controlled dose of what would normally be harmful becomes the mechanism of repair.

By surviving the Moab 240, I recalibrated my body's threat-detection system to a level no amount of office stress management could reach. My nervous system now understands what genuine danger feels like: the cold, the dark, running on broken feet, unable to eat without vomiting. Consequently, the code-red alarms of daily business life get downgraded. Not through attitude or discipline. Through biological data.

When I returned to work, the change was immediate and specific.

An unexpected financial hit, a difficult personnel situation, a client crisis at six in the evening: my body no longer dumps cortisol into the bloodstream. The noise floor has dropped. What used to constitute a crisis now barely registers, because my nervous system has a new reference point for what crisis actually is.

> *Most leaders are porous, leaking energy into every obstacle that crosses their path. By voluntarily facing the abyss, you become dense. You raise the threshold of what constitutes a crisis so high that the daily friction of business barely registers.*

Endurance athletes typically carry a biological age that is 10 to 15 years younger than their chronological age. This is not a side effect of the training. It is the result of deliberate stress, applied with intention and survived.

The mechanism is measurable. Telomeres are the protective caps on chromosomes that prevent them from fraying: the shoelace cap of your genetic material. Under chronic passive stress, they shorten. Under acute voluntary stress followed by recovery, they hold. Elizabeth Blackburn won the Nobel Prize for demonstrating this. The biology of what you choose to endure is not the same as the biology of what you are forced to absorb.

Going into Moab at 55, my measured biological age was 31. It has since moved to 39 as my training load has lightened. I include these numbers not to impress you. I include them because the gap between what the calendar says and what the cells say is the physical record of every hard thing I chose.

Worried to death is a well-known phrase. It's real. The ambient anxiety of the office ages us. Chosen stress, practiced and controlled, pays back the debt.

The Protocol of the Wild

When the modern executive hears "vision quest," they picture crystals and mild discomfort in a comfortable tent. This is a sanitization of history. Historically, a vision quest was not a retreat. It was a calculated brush with death, designed to ensure that the boy who entered did not come back, and the man who returned was someone the tribe could trust with its survival.

What is remarkable, looking at these rites across cultures with no connection to one another, is how consistent the architecture is. Geography, language, and mythology differed. The core mechanism did not.

Figure 5.2: Vision Quest Examples

The ordeal does not have a fixed form.
What it requires is fixed: that it costs enough to matter, and that you finish it.

Tradition	Culture	Core Mechanism
Crypteia	Sparta, Greece	Youth sent into the wild with nothing but a knife. Radical self-reliance; all status and tools stripped away.
Hanbleceya	Lakota, US	"Crying for a Vision." The Seeker was left in a pit or on a cliff edge without food or water for four days. Confronting the terrifying silence of the ego.
Yamabushi Shugendo	Japan	Mountain monks hanging over cliff edges, standing under freezing waterfalls. Ending the chatterbox ego through extreme physical shock.
Walkabout	Aboriginal Australian	Months-long rite of separation, navigating the vast outback via Songlines. Transitioning from theoretical knowledge to visceral self-reliance.
Moran	Maasai, Kenya & Tanzania	Transition to warrior status required stalking a lion

		with only a spear. Overcoming the primal fear of death to serve the community as a protector.

Every one of these traditions was built on the same principle: the social mask has to die before the leader can be born. The comfortable identity, the one that knows where it stands in the hierarchy and what its status is, cannot survive the ordeal intact. That is not a flaw in the design. It is the design.

The Architecture of the Quest

Regardless of geography, every vision quest follows the same three-part structure that Joseph Campbell identified across the world's mythologies. If your challenge does not hit all three, it is not a quest. It is a holiday.

1. Separation

You must leave the known world. You cannot quest in your living room. The cord to ordinary life must be genuinely severed, not just loosened. In a leadership context, this means killing the pings. You cannot find your center while you are tethered to the inbox. Separation also proves something essential: that the organization can survive your temporary absence. That proof matters. It is the first crack in the illusion that you are indispensable.

2. Ordeal (Liminality)

You enter the unknown. You face hunger, cold, fatigue, fear, or all of them. This is where the social mask begins to dissolve, not through reflection but through depletion. As glucose reserves fall and the Default Mode Network, the chatterbox ego that worries about status and emails, begins to power down, the brain enters hypofrontality. The biological door to genuine insight. You cannot think your way to a vision. You have to exhaust the body to free the mind.

For me, that moment arrived on day three, not as a revelation exactly, but as a kind of cellular clarity. My world condensed to a single understanding: the act of turning on a tap and having clean water come out is all I need. Everything else is surplus. That knowledge did not arrive as a thought. It arrived as a physical fact, felt in the body at a level that has not left me since.

3. Return

You come back. But you are not the same person who left, and that is the whole point. The Return is the most dangerous phase for leaders, because it is where most of the value is lost. If you walk back through the office door and resume the old habits within forty-eight hours, the quest was expensive time off. Nothing more.

The Return is about translation: taking the clarity you earned in the desert and using it to rebuild the inner architecture of how you lead. You return as the angel who provides safety, because you have now mastered the fire. You know what you are capable of under pressure because you have been under pressure that has no floor.

The Hard Call

The Inner Citadel is a construction project. Most people spend their lives decorating the outside of their houses while the foundations are made of sand.

I did not pick the Moab because I was good at it. I picked it because I was certain it would break the person I thought I was. If you only quest in areas where you are already strong, you are not building a Citadel. You are redecorating a room you already own.

Find the thing that makes your stomach turn. The one that feels beyond you. Go into that discomfort and stay until the ego falls and the Citadel rises. That is not a metaphor. It is the oldest instruction manual in human history, and it has been road-tested across every culture that ever built something worth keeping.

> *You have to select something that scares you and feels beyond you. To break ground so you can be rebuilt.*

Chapter Tool: The Citadel Audit

Three questions. Answer them honestly before moving to the next chapter.

Figure 5.3: The Citadel Audit

Before you can rebuild, you need an honest account of what has eroded. Use this to find out where you actually are.

The Lintel	Who is the 'Pocket Rocket' in your life? What hard thing forged their Inner Citadel?
The Leak	Where is your Citadel wall currently crumbling? Is it digital noise, a lack of physical evidence of your own strength, or something else?
The Descent	Are you ready to stop decorating the rooms you own and start breaking ground on a foundation that doesn't move?

Figure 5.4: Your Inner Citadel
Not a metaphor. A structure you build, deliberately, through the accumulation of hard choices made and kept.

Further Resources & References

Anterior Midcingulate Cortex (aMCC): Dr. Andrew Huberman and David Goggins discuss the aMCC and the neuroscience of building willpower. YouTube, Huberman Lab.

Epigenetics and endurance: DNA methylation studies in ultra-endurance athletes reveal rapid changes in gene expression governing inflammation, metabolism, and cellular repair.

Telomere research: Elizabeth Blackburn and Elissa Epel, The Telomere Effect: A Revolutionary Approach to Living Younger, Healthier, Longer.

Vision Quest tradition: David Courchene on Vision Quests. YouTube: https://www.youtube.com/watch?v=SjWquvl6KvY

Joseph Campbell (1904-1987): The Hero with a Thousand Faces. Comparative mythologist who formalized the three-part hero's journey structure (departure, initiation, return).

Arnold van Gennep (1873-1957): coined 'rites of passage.' His three-part ritual structure (separation, transition, incorporation) underpins Campbell's framework.

Inner Citadel: Stoic concept, central to Marcus Aurelius's Meditations. The internal fortress of the mind that no external adversity can penetrate.

CHAPTER 6 - WHY WE NEED VISION QUESTS MORE THAN EVER

After ten or twenty years of building a career, most people construct lives optimized for comfort: the house, the car, the mortgage, the holidays, the carefully managed diet and wardrobe. On the surface, it looks like success. Underneath, it can become a velvet prison.

We compromise in small ways that compound. Working alongside people we quietly resent. Accepting conditions we would not have accepted ten years ago. Collecting a thousand paper cuts in exchange for stability. The lifestyle that was meant to protect us slowly softens us. We lose our edge. We lose the memory of what we were capable of when the stakes were real.

Our children, early career adults raised in this comfort, also become locked in padded prisons created by their parents. Without deliberate intervention, a human being can remain in a state of psychological adolescence indefinitely. Biology guarantees that we age. Culture determines whether we mature. To become a leader, a protector, an elder, the child self must eventually relinquish power. It never does so willingly. That is precisely why ancient cultures did not leave this transition to chance. They engineered it.

> *A few generations ago, scarcity performed the work that comfort now avoids. Survival required effort, and effort built meaning. The transition to adulthood was not symbolic. It demanded proof.*

Families fixed what broke. Clothes were handed down. Treats were earned. Because nothing was guaranteed, every small luxury was felt with intensity: a slice of cake, a new coat, a warm house in winter. Children grew up understanding sacrifice, dreaming of a better future, and taking risks to reach it.

That world did not produce perfect people. But it produced initiated ones—people who had been tested and knew it. Today, experienced career adults and their children entering the workplace need to re-up.

The Threshold

Anthropologist Victor Turner called the in-between state of transformation liminality, from the Latin limen: threshold. It is the condition of being neither what you were nor what you will become. In traditional rites of passage, the initiate temporarily loses status. They are not a child but not yet an adult. Stripped of identity, they stand in a psychological doorway.

Out in the desert, away from the city, you discover very quickly how thin your armor actually is. Titles vanish. Roles disappear. You are reduced to flesh, bone, and whatever is underneath. When the armor falls away, what remains is undeniable.

What the Desert Found

At Moab, I sobbed. I could not stop it.

Beginning late on the second day, it came three or four times daily: sudden, uncontrollable waves. I am not an emotional person. My family jokes that I don't even register excitement. I built my life around seriousness, around paying the bills and protecting stability. Crying is not part of that identity.

But somewhere around mile 140, biology overruled identity. Sleep deprivation and exhaustion shut down the prefrontal cortex, the part of the brain that maintains the professional mask. What surfaced was not sadness. It was awe. A dismantling of ego so complete that there was nothing left to perform.

Ultra-runners talk about this. When the body is stripped to its limits, perspective shifts. You realize how small you are, how hard life truly is, and how miraculous it is that you are still moving forward. Paradoxically, being reduced to nothing feels expansive. Alone with only your own capacity to survive, gratitude becomes physical. Wonder returns. The luxury of everyday life, usually invisible, becomes radiant in its absence.

The sobbing did not feel like weakness. It felt like something unnecessary leaving the body. A recognition of fragility and resilience existing in the same moment, in the same person, at the same time.

> *Beneath the armor, beneath the comfort, there is a core that is far tougher than we remember. The ordeal does not install it. It uncovers it.*

Lines in the Sand

Humans need thresholds. We need distinct lines that say: before this, I was one person. After this, I am another.

Before the Moab 240, I was complicit in my own suffocation. After the Moab 240, I was exactly the person I wanted to be. Not because the race gave me something new. Because it stripped away everything that was not actually me.

A threshold without friction is just a change of scenery. You have to break ground on your biology before you can be rebuilt on it. For some, that threshold is a seven-day fast. For others, it is a summit attempt, a silent retreat, a cold-water season, an extended period of deliberate solitude. The form is less important than the function: it must be genuinely hard, genuinely voluntary, and long enough that the ego runs out of things to say.

By choosing the hard path, you perform high-repetition training for the Anterior Midcingulate Cortex. You physically thicken the part of the brain responsible for tenacity. The biology changes. Then the identity follows. In that order, and not the other way around.

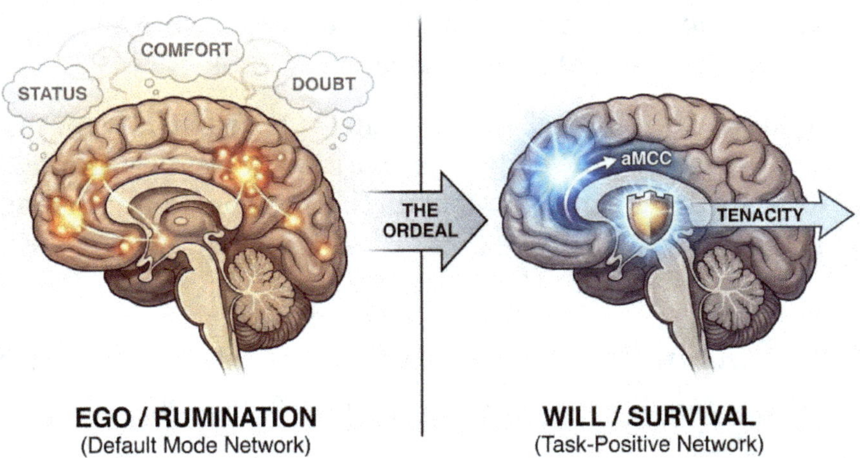

Figure 6.1: The Anterior Midcingulate Cortex: The Root of Will
The part of the brain that grows when you do things you don't want to do. Voluntary hardship is not psychological; it is anatomical.

The Uninitiated Running the World

The deeper crisis is not personal. It is structural.

We have deleted the ordeal from modern life, and the consequence is a world run by uninitiated adults: people who wield authority without ever having tested their own breaking point. Leaders who manage risk without having genuinely encountered it. Executives who make decisions about other people's sacrifice without having paid any themselves.

When a leader builds an Inner Citadel through a genuine ordeal, something changes in how they hold power. They stop being transactional and start being protective. They lead differently. They know something different: that the comfort they are protecting for others is worth protecting, because they know what its absence feels like.

The evidence for this is not only personal. Studies on national service, structured challenge programs, and community-based rites of passage consistently show measurable improvements in social cohesion, civic engagement, psychological well-being, and long-term economic mobility. These are not soft outcomes. They are the measurable byproducts of people who have been tested and returned.

Vision quests are not just good for the individual who undertakes them. They are the civic infrastructure that rebuilds collective resilience. More people who have earned their place the hard way hold each other, and all of us, together.

> *We haven't just lost the ordeal from individual lives. We have lost it from the culture. And the culture has become exactly as fragile as you would expect.*

Chapter Tool: The Threshold Audit

Three questions. Answer them with the same honesty the desert demands.

Figure 6.2: The Threshold Audit
A threshold without friction is just a change of scenery.

The Nameless Moment	When was the last time you were truly without title, status, or role? What did you find there?
The Trailhead	What is the hard thing currently making your stomach turn? That discomfort is not a warning. It is a direction.
The Ground	Are you decorating a room you already own, or are you ready to break ground on a Citadel that does not yet exist?

Further Resources & References

Liminality: Victor Turner, The Ritual Process: Structure and Anti-Structure (1969). The concept of liminality as a threshold state between identities.

Social cohesion: The Contact Hypothesis in National Service. Brookings Institution. brookings.edu/articles/national-service-can-connect-americas-young-people-to-opportunity-and-community

Social cohesion: Intergroup Marriage and Mandatory Service Study (Sweden, 2012).

Civic engagement: AmeriCorps Longitudinal Study, 1999-2007. Corporation for National and Community Service.

Civic engagement: The Civic Consciousness Natural Experiment (France, Post-Conscription Analysis).

Public health: Adolescent Volunteering and Subsequent Health and Well-Being. JAMA Network Open, 2023. https://jamanetwork.com/journals/jamanetworkopen/fullarticle/2805474

Public health: Finnish Defense Forces Health Longitudinal Study.

Economic mobility: 2025 State of Alums Report. Service Year Alliance. serviceyearalliance.org

Economic mobility: The Economic Value of National Service. Voices for National Service.

Career outcomes: LISC AmeriCorps Member Outcome Study. Urban Institute, 2020.

Career outcomes: Military Service and Economic Mobility: Evidence from the Civil War. Lee, 2012.

CHAPTER 7 - YOUR ENVIRONMENT IS IN YOU

Parts I and II made the case. Part III is the method. But before you can design your own ordeal, you need to understand something that most leadership books miss entirely: your environment is not around you. It is in you. And it has been rewriting you for years.

I was running along the American River near Sacramento in 2013, tracking along a high cliff trail, when an American Eagle pulled alongside me.

Figure 7.1: The American River, Sacramento
What your nervous system is designed for. Not the screen, not the open-plan office, this.

It flew at my shoulder for what was probably two minutes and felt like two hours. Neither of us adjusted course. It did not seem alarmed by my presence, and I found I was not thinking about anything at all: not pace, not the race, not the next decision waiting for me on a screen. I was simply there, moving through the same air as a bird that weighed nothing and could go anywhere.

When I finished the run, I understood something I had not been able to articulate before: I had not been running through the environment. I had been part of it.

I tattooed the image on my side. Not as a trophy. As a reminder of what it feels like to be complete. And to remind me to return.

> *I spent decades as a Head in a Jar: convinced that my mind was a closed loop, my environment merely a backdrop, and that willpower and Wi-Fi were sufficient infrastructure for a life. I was wrong.*

The science of embodied cognition has confirmed what that morning on the American River made me feel: we do not just live in our environment. We are a continuation of it. We are porous. We are constantly exchanging energy, microbes, and biological signals with what I call the Original Stack: the natural world for which our hardware was actually designed.

The Original Stack

The stack has five layers.

The light layer. We are designed to track the sun's arc across the day. Full-spectrum natural light regulates cortisol, melatonin, and circadian timing in ways that no artificial lighting system replicates. The body is a sundial. It needs the sun to know what time it is.

The thermal layer. We are built to experience temperature as a variable, not a setting. The body's stress-response and recovery systems require cold and heat to cycle properly. A life maintained at 72 degrees is a thermostat, not a nervous system.

The microbiome layer. We are porous organisms, designed to sample and be part of the earth, the plants, and the living systems around us. Environmental porosity is not a metaphor. It is a biological process. The immune system learns from what it encounters. Sterilize the environment completely, and you sterilize the education.

The fractal layer. The human visual system is calibrated to the geometric patterns of the natural world: branching trees, coastlines, and moving water. These fractal patterns measurably reduce physiological stress. Straight lines and right angles do not. The modern office is geometrically hostile.

The gravity and grounding layer. We are built to feel the unevenness of the earth beneath us and to move across varied terrain. The sensory feedback of uneven ground activates postural and neurological systems that a flat floor and an ergonomic chair permanently suppress.

When you ignore the stack, you are not just stressed. You are biologically out of sync. The digital fog that disconnects us from completeness as organisms is the same fog that disconnects us from the depth of thought. They are the same problem. The solution in both cases is the same: reconnect the hardware to the environment it was built for.

This chapter is not an argument for living in the woods. It is an argument for understanding what happens, at the cellular and neurological level, when you step into nature, and what you are losing every hour you spend without it.

The Chemical Handshake

When I stand in the forest at my upstate New York Retreat Center, I am not relaxing. I am engaged in a high-level chemical exchange.

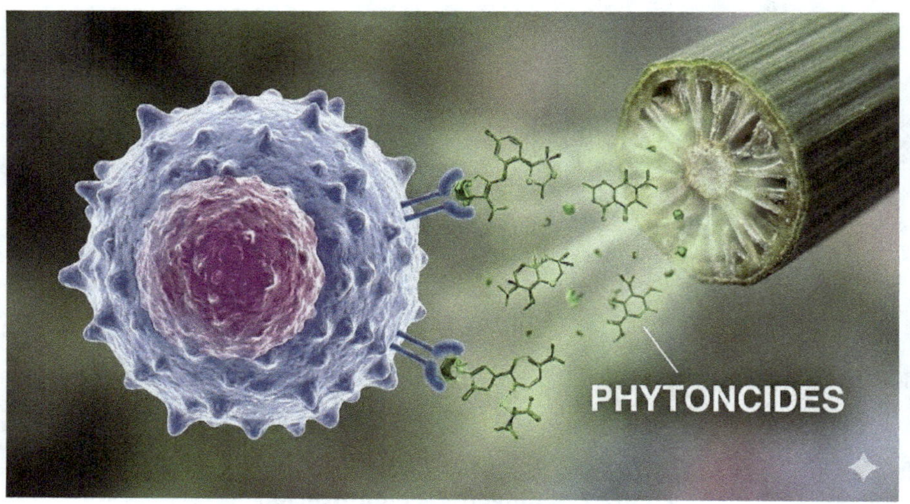

Figure 7.2: Phytoncides
The chemical handshake between forest and human. The data on how immersion in natural environments affects cortisol, NK cells, and cognitive recovery are not soft science.

Trees are not passive scenery. To protect themselves from rot and insects, they emit antimicrobial organic compounds called phytoncides. When we inhale these compounds, they bind to receptors on our immune cells and trigger a significant increase in the activity of Natural Killer cells: the front-line soldiers of the immune system. Research by immunologist Qing Li and his team found that a single weekend in a forest environment led to increases in NK cells that persisted for more than 30 days.

In the Original Stack, the trees are actively updating your biology. In a glass-and-drywall office, that handshake never happens. Your immune system is waiting for a signal that the environment no longer sends.

The Environment Rewrites the Hardware

The most structurally important proof of our porous nature is epigenetics, introduced in Chapter 5. Here, it bears a specific application.

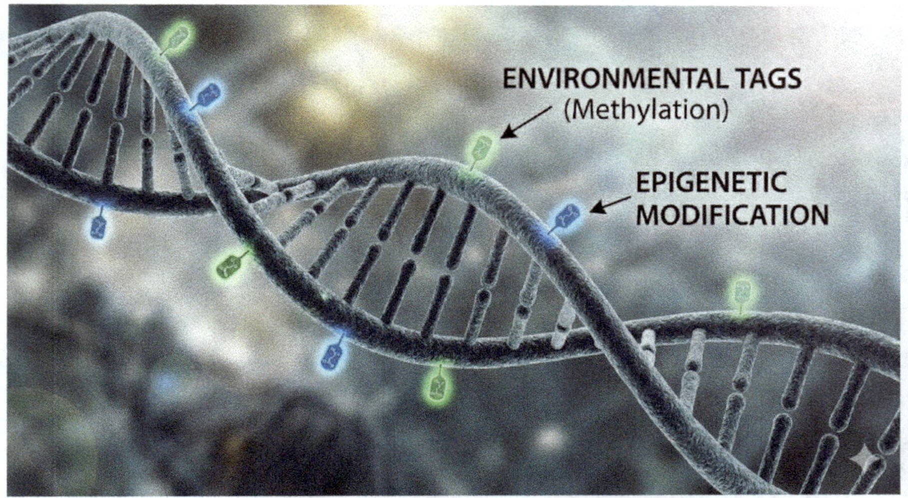

Figure 7.3: Epigenetic Modification
Voluntary hardship does not just change your mind. It changes what your genes express. The update is biological, and it persists.

Your DNA is not a fixed blueprint. It is a dynamic script being edited in real time by your surroundings. The quality of light, the presence or absence of synthetic noise, the physical demands of a mountain environment: all of these send chemical signals that attach methyl groups to specific genes, turning expression up or down. When you place yourself in a demanding natural environment, you signal your biology to express resilience. When you remain in a climate-controlled office, you send a different signal: that the body no longer needs to be strong because nothing will ever require it to be. This is even worse for those already suffering from chronic stress, where their fight or flight response never gets to turn off.

Your environment is not shaping your mood. It is shaping your hardware.

Fractal Fluency

Have you noticed that looking at a profit-and-loss statement for an hour gives you a headache, while looking at a forest for an hour brings clarity? The difference is not subjective. It is mathematical.

Figure 7.4: Fractal Fluency
The visual geometry of nature that the human nervous system recognizes as home. Why the wilderness works on you even before you understand how.

Our visual system is biologically tuned to a specific geometric quality found throughout the natural world: fractals. The branching of a tree, the edge of a cloud, and the veining of a leaf all follow fractal dimensions that precisely match the neural architecture of the human retina. When the eye processes fractal patterns, stress response measurably drops. Research by physicist Richard Taylor found reductions in physiological stress markers of up to sixty percent through fractal viewing alone.

In the city, we are surrounded by straight lines and right angles. These shapes do not exist in the Original Stack. The brain has to work harder simply to process the environment, a condition researchers call Directed Attention Fatigue. We are not failing to concentrate. We are spending our concentration budget on the cognitive overhead of living in an environment our visual system was not built for.

Clearing the Cache

There is a specific kind of depletion that no amount of sleep fully repairs. You know it. The Sunday morning after a week of back-to-back decisions, when rest has technically happened but something essential is still empty. Directed attention, the willed, effortful focus required for strategy, legal review, and difficult personnel conversations, is a finite biological resource. When it runs out, the symptoms look like character failures: irritability, poor decisions, reduced empathy. They are not failures of character. They are failures of supply.

Rachel and Stephen Kaplan at the University of Michigan identified the restoration mechanism in their Attention Restoration Theory. Directed attention cannot restore itself through rest alone. It restores through a qualitatively different mode of engagement they called soft fascination: the involuntary, effortless attention captured by moving water, wind through trees, the shifting light on a hillside. When these stimuli hold the eye and mind, the directed attention circuitry goes offline entirely. Not suppressed. Not merely resting. Genuinely offline, recharging, without the act of will that the office demands.

This is the precise mechanism by which the vision quest works on a dimension the corporate retreat cannot reach. The retreat removes the workload. The wilderness removes the cognitive overhead entirely. Four days in the desert, with no dashboard to check, and no inbox to manage, is not four days of rest. It is four days of the directed attention system being given genuine permission to stop. The capacity that returns on day five is not the same as the capacity depleted on day one. It is restored to a baseline that the executive has not felt in years.

> *You don't go into the woods to hide from your problems. You go to become the person capable of solving them.*

The Convergence

Four separate bodies of science: immunology, epigenetics, visual neuroscience, and cognitive psychology. Four different mechanisms. One consistent finding.

The human organism was built for a specific environment, and it performs best in proximity to that environment. The Original Stack is not nostalgia for nature. It is the operating condition for which the hardware was designed. Every hour spent in artificial light, synthetic noise, and fractal-free geometry is an hour spent running the machine outside its design parameters.

The vision quest does not ask you to abandon the world you operate in. It asks you to remember what you are made of. To return, deliberately and at sufficient depth, to the environment that built you. So that you carry something of it back.

Part III begins here. It is time to choose your quest and conduct it.

Chapter Tool: The Sensory Audit

Five questions. Answer honestly before reading the consequence.

Figure 7.5: The Sensory Audit

What your environment is currently doing to your nervous system, measured against what it needs.

The Friction Check	Does your daily environment require constant hard attention or vigilance? Traffic, notifications, synthetic noise. How many hours each day are you spending in that state?
The Fractal Gap	When did you last spend an hour looking at a pattern that a marketing team or a product manager did not design?
The Sync Question	Is your body currently calibrated to a drywall box or the rising sun? What would it take to change that for one week?
The Consequence	*You cannot lead a world you are out of sync with. Recalibrate the environment, and the mind follows.*

Further Resources & References

Phytoncides and NK cells: Qing Li, Effect of forest bathing trips on human immune function. Environmental Health and Preventive Medicine, 2010. NK cells increase persisting 30+ days after forest immersion.

Fractal stress reduction: Richard Taylor, University of Oregon. Fractal fluency research shows up to a 60% reduction in physiological stress markers through viewing fractal patterns.

Attention Restoration Theory: Rachel and Stephen Kaplan, The Experience of Nature (1989). Directed attention as a finite resource; soft fascination as the restoration mechanism.

Directed Attention Fatigue: Kaplan & Kaplan. Effortful attention depletion in built environments: involuntary attention as the recovery pathway.

Epigenetics and environmental signaling: see Chapter 5 references. DNA methylation in response to physical environment, light quality, and stress exposure.

Embodied cognition: Francisco Varela, Evan Thompson, Eleanor Rosch, The Embodied Mind (1991). The body-environment system is the unit of cognition, not the brain in isolation.

PART III - THE ROOT ASTRO QUEST METHOD

CHAPTER 8 - FIVE STAGES OF VOLUNTARY HARDSHIP AND RETURN

Before I explain the method, I want you to do something. Find a quiet spot. Close your eyes. Now imagine someone you love is in immediate, physical danger. A threat is standing in front of them. You are the only person who can intervene. You have to act now.

Sit with that feeling for thirty seconds.

What happened?

Most likely: the to-do list vanished. The impostor syndrome vanished. The ambient anxiety about the quarterly review vanished. What replaced all of it was a cold spike in the gut. Your amygdala slammed the override switch. Your heart began to hammer with a heavy, rhythmic thud. Your vision constricted. Every watt of cognitive energy redirected to a single point.

You entered a state of Biological Salience. Your body traded the frantic, thin energy of the drift for the dense, heavy fuel of hardened will. You were not thinking about your purpose. You were physically incapable of thinking about anything else.

> *This is the state the Root Astro Quest Method is designed to access. Not by manufacturing a crisis, but by creating the conditions under which that quality of attention returns naturally, and stays.*

High-Speed Drift

The reason that simulation landed is that you recognize its opposite.

You know the feeling: back-to-back meetings, an inbox that regenerates faster than you can clear it, decisions made at speed with insufficient information, and at the end of a twelve-hour day, the specific exhaustion of someone who has been moving at pace in no particular direction. You are steering, but the car is sliding. I call this state High-Speed Drift.

Modern leaders do not lack intelligence, ambition, or opportunity. What they increasingly lack is orientation. We know how to move fast. We do not always know where we are going. We know how to optimize. We do not always know what matters. We are connected to everything: markets, teams, trends, notifications. Yet we are grounded in quicksand.

The Root Astro Quest Method exists to address this specific condition. It is a temporary return to the circumstances under which human clarity evolved, followed by a deliberate return to leadership with greater calm, resilience, and truth.

Why Root Astro

The name is deliberate. It holds two inverse and complementary forces in a single instrument.

Root: To stabilize, we must go down. We must reconnect with the root systems: our biology, the physical world, nature, and the ancient hard-wiring of the nervous system. A tree without deep roots cannot survive a storm, no matter how tall it grows.

Astrolabe (Astro): An ancient navigational instrument used to calculate position relative to the stars. It was a tool of orientation in a vast, featureless ocean. We are currently adrift in a digital ocean with no landmarks. The Root Astro Quest Method is a method for finding your coordinates again: to move with the stars, the eternal truths, rather than the waves, the daily noise.

Every culture that has survived long enough to pass on its wisdom has understood this pattern. The Aboriginal Walkabout, the Native American Vision Quest, the Buddhist forest retreat, the Stoic practice of voluntary discomfort: these are not primitive rituals from less sophisticated times. They are proven methods for recalibration, refined over millennia, designed to solve a problem that affluent modern life has made epidemic: the slow erosion of the self under conditions of unrelenting comfort and digital saturation.

The Root Astro Quest Method

The method does not borrow or replicate Indigenous ceremonies. It honors the pattern, not the ritual. The pattern is universal, repeatable, and deeply human.

Figure 8.1: The Root Astro Quest Method

Five stages. Not a self-help framework. A structured recalibration protocol built on neuroscience, anthropology, and direct proof.

#	Stage	Function
1	**Realization**	breaks denial
2	**Severance**	breaks habit

3	**Descent**	breaks illusion
4	**Revelation**	reveals truth
5	**Return**	builds a new life

Five stages. One arc. This is not ancient mysticism. It is human recalibration.

Stage One / The Realization
The signal you have been suppressing

Every vision quest begins long before anyone steps into the wilderness. It begins with an uncomfortable, often quiet recognition: something essential is eroding.

There is a neurological basis for this. The brain's reward circuitry adapts to constant comfort through hedonic adaptation: the mechanism by which yesterday's luxury becomes today's baseline. When everything is available on demand, dopamine responses flatten. What once produced genuine satisfaction no longer registers. The problem is not ingratitude. The problem is that the nervous system was optimized for a world of scarcity, and abundance without friction leaves it with nothing to calibrate against.

For me, it wasn't a sudden crash. It was a slow rot.

It was the realization that I was tolerating behaviors & methods of working I hated because the financial lock-in was too good. That I was optimizing my life and losing myself in the process. My leadership style is as close to the silverback gorilla in chapter 3 as you can get. I collaborate, but I have to lead & protect. Making myself smaller to serve a bigger need works for a while. It does not work for long. My sense of who I was, was too large to survive indefinitely in a space that required a smaller version of me.

That is ego, yes. But ego is not simply vanity. It is the identity we have built, for better or worse. There are parts of it we should hold onto. Parts instilled in us by our parents in the early years that we should interrogate. Parts born of ignorance that colleagues and partners can chip away at and reshape. My wife chips away at mine constantly, revealing something better underneath, as do my daughters. My colleagues, especially our founders at the venture builder I work for, are incredibly smart with feedback, baked into their organization's culture for decades.

But some parts are non-negotiable. I am discerning enough to know which is which.

I chose silverback. Hard and kind. Protective and brave for the teams and family in my care.

My mother's standing instruction was: "Take shit off no one." My father would look gangs of drug dealers in the eye at our pub and say, "Fuck off. You're not coming in." And I was compromising myself for a few dollars more. That had to change.

Stage One is the courage to listen to the signal. To stop numbing and say: This isn't working. I need a reset.

For you, the realization might look different:

- The Hollow Success: you hit your numbers and feel nothing. The work, the team, the why, is not where you are meant to be.
- The Fog: You sit in strategy meetings and realize you have no original thoughts left, only reactions.
- The Short Fuse: you snap at the people closest to you because your nervous system is running at its ceiling.

Most leaders spend years suppressing this stage. A new car. A changed job. A temporary project. Something to suppress the signal and avoid the truth. We are not supposed to be doing this. Stage One is the moment you stop pretending.

Stage Two / The Severance
Cutting the cord

Insight without separation is impossible. You cannot recalibrate a compass while standing next to a magnet. The magnet, in our case, is the digital environment: the identity-reinforcing context of every role, every expectation, every notification that tells you who you are supposed to be.

Research on attention residue, studied by Sophie Leroy at the University of Washington, shows that even a glance at an email leaves a cognitive trace that persists for twenty minutes or more. This is not a productivity problem. It is a recalibration problem. Full severance is not a philosophical stance. It is a physiological precondition for the cognitive state that the method requires.

Consider what your digital devices actually carry.

If you have your phone, you are a CEO.

If you have your email, you are a Manager.

If you have your likes, you are a Brand.

To find out what you are without all of that, you have to put it down.

The Severance Protocol

- Digital Amputation: non-negotiable. Phones, laptops, and watches are surrendered. You must be unreachable. The brain needs to register that no help is coming and no distraction is available.
- Role Suspension: You leave your title at the trailhead. In the

wilderness, you are not a VP. You are a mammal that requires water and shelter.

- Physical Departure: You must leave your home, your office, and your familiar comforts. Distance is functional, not symbolic.

I remember the specific moment this landed during my Moab preparation. Six months of training, and then a week before the race, I went to the snow-covered mountains near Salt Lake City to get some altitude training into my lungs. Staying in a small cabin, simple hiking, and gentle runs in nature daily. Computer and phone off. Reading and centering my mind for the ordeal ahead. The weight of what I was not carrying was immediately physical. Not relief. More like amputation. Which was, of course, precisely the point.

What Severance creates is the liminality threshold we introduced in Chapter 6: the state of being neither what you were nor what you are becoming. You are no longer a CEO. You are not yet whatever comes next. The old identity is suspended, and the new one has not yet formed. It is an uncomfortable place to stand.

Victor Turner described liminality as a deliberate dissolution of social structure that allows new structures to emerge. In practical terms: you cannot redesign the architecture of a building while you are still living inside it. The building has to come down first. That is what Severance does.

The discomfort of the liminal state is the mechanism, not the side effect. During Moab training and the race itself, the liminality felt like a horror film with no exits. Looking back, it was the moment the better version became possible.

One consequence of shared liminality is worth naming here. When people move through it together, as soldiers do in basic training or students in a cohort, the removal of status produces what Turner called communitas: intense, ego-less bonds formed in the absence of hierarchy. Because no one carries their title, everyone is equal. For leadership teams undertaking Root Astro strategic retreats together, this is one of our methods' most powerful and least expected outcomes.

Stage Three / The Descent

The ordeal

This is the heart of the method.

The Descent is the period of voluntary hardship: solitude, physical effort, sensory simplification, and sustained discomfort. In the Moab 240, mine was extended to physical brutality. Hallucinations for days. The complete collapse of the ego under the accumulated weight of sleep deprivation and pain. Your Descent does not have to be 240 miles. But it has to be hard.

It must include three elements.

- Solitude: no talking, no podcasts, no input. Just the deafening sound of your own mind, unmediated.
- Nature: vast, indifferent landscapes that recalibrate your sense of scale.
- Effort: hiking, fasting, surviving the elements, or simply enduring for longer than feels reasonable.

The mechanism is both psychological and physiological. Under sustained discomfort, the prefrontal cortex, responsible for planning, social performance, and narrative construction, gradually loses its grip. The social mask, the part of you that monitors how you appear and manages what you project, begins to fall. When it falls, something rawer emerges: pattern recognition, emotional processing, somatic awareness. The constant inner monologue that executives mistake for thinking is often just the prefrontal cortex defending existing beliefs. The Descent quiets that defense.

The difficulty of this state is the sensation of synaptic rewiring. In the liminal space of genuine hardship, the brain increases production of Brain-Derived Neurotrophic Factor: BDNF, the Miracle-Gro of neuroplasticity. The hardship creates the heat necessary to break old neural patterns. The liminal state provides a window when neurons are most receptive to forming new, more resilient connections.

In short, you have to break the model of yourself before you can update it. The Descent is the process of clearing the old code.

Internal narratives surface as the prefrontal cortex stops suppressing them. Unresolved fears emerge. Priorities reorder themselves without effort. The quarterly report stops mattering. The temperature of the air starts to.

> *The Descent is not punishment. It is exfoliation. It scrubs away the dead layers of the self so the fresh skin can breathe.*

Stage Four / **The Revelation**

The quiet signal

Revelation is rarely fireworks. It is rarely a burning bush. It is usually quiet, simple, and undeniable. After enough noise has been removed through Severance, and the ego has been exhausted through Descent, something true finally has room to speak.

On day two in the desert, a freak storm brought heavy rain for most of the day. I spent hours slogging through deep mud with nothing to do but think. At some point, with no screen to check and no meeting to prepare for, my mind went somewhere it had been avoiding for years: the arithmetic of whatever time I had left, and what actually deserved to occupy it.

The words and actions of people that had become enormous irritants were, from out there, dust specks. I would be on this planet for perhaps another thirty birthdays. That was it, if I was lucky.

What followed was not anger at the people who had been irritating me. It was something more uncomfortable. The irritants were not the problem. I had been choosing to stay in situations that required me to be smaller than I was, and blaming my discomfort with that choice on someone else. That was the thing to fix.

I committed there and then: these small things would no longer get that space. Not because I had forgiven them. Because I had more important things to do with my time.

On day three, the revelation was simpler and went deeper.

Clean water. That was it.

The visceral, cellular understanding that clean water equals wealth, and everything else in my life, the warm house, the food delivered to my phone, the weekend trips, the endless choices, was complete luxury. If you have clean water, you have time to build shelter and find food. If you do not have clean water, nothing else matters. That understanding did not arrive as a thought. It arrived as a fact the body already knew and had simply never been given the conditions to say.

That clarity became the seed for everything I did next.

> *A true revelation has gravitational pull. You don't think it. You know it. It is the compass needle finally settling North.*

Modern culture has industrialized the concept of the breakthrough. Every leadership retreat promises transformation by Friday afternoon. But genuine revelation, the kind that actually changes behavior, is not consumed. It is earned. It arrives after the ego has been exhausted, not stimulated. The difference between a conference insight and a revelation forged in hardship is the difference between reading about fire and being burned. One informs. The other transforms.

Revelations commonly take the form of:

- I am doing work that is too small for me.
- I am not living enough in service of others, and want to do more
- I am leading from compromise, not from conviction.

Stage Five / The Return

The reintegration

This is where most modern retreats fail.

You have the insight. You feel rebuilt. Then you return to the office on Monday, open four hundred emails, and by Tuesday, the insight is a memory rather than a change. The pattern is depressingly predictable: a leader has a profound experience, a retreat, a sabbatical, a health scare. They return determined to change. Within seventy-two hours, the inbox has re-established its tyranny, the calendar has filled, and the nervous system has re-adapted to its prior tempo. The insight fades. The old identity reasserts itself. And the experience becomes a story told at dinner parties rather than a foundation built upon.

Insight without integration is just nostalgia.

In the Root Astro Quest Method, the Return is a structured ninety-day process with three components.

- The Code of Return: before leaving the wilderness, you write your non-negotiables. What are you going to stop? What are you going to start? Written, not remembered.
- The Depth of Presence: you plan nature, movement, and the deep, important strategic projects that create 'Communitas' led by you, both social and in work.

- The New Identity: you return not as the person who left, but as the person who survived. You carry the authority of the ordeal and the method, plan, and mindset to maintain it.

At Root Astro, we build specific accountability structures around this: an integration plan completed before leaving the wilderness, a thirty-day re-entry protocol with daily practices, a structured ninety-day check-in, and a community of others who have completed the method and can hold each other to the standard set during your practice.

The goal is not to escape from modern life. It is mastery of it. To return, able to engage the world without being consumed by it. To lead without chronic anxiety. To choose hard things before life chooses them for you.

The Method as a Whole

Figure 8.2: The Method as a Whole

The complete architecture. Each stage has a function; none is optional; the sequence is the point.

#	Stage	Function
1	**Realization**	breaks denial
2	**Severance**	breaks habit
3	**Descent**	breaks illusion
4	**Revelation**	reveals truth
5	**Return**	builds a new life

Taken together, the five stages form a single arc of deliberate recalibration. Each stage does specific work that the next stage depends on. You cannot have a genuine Revelation without the Descent. You cannot complete the Descent without the Severance. You cannot begin the Severance without the Realization.

The stages are not interchangeable. They are sequential. That is the architecture.

> *The Ordeal is not ancient mysticism. It is a structured return to the conditions under which human clarity has always been found. A way back to what is real.*

Further Resources & References

Hedonic adaptation: Frederick & Loewenstein (1999). The mechanism by which repeated positive experiences produce diminishing returns in subjective well-being.

Attention residue: Sophie Leroy, University of Washington. 'Why Is It So Hard to Do My Work?' (2009). Cognitive traces from task-switching persist for up to 23 minutes.

Liminality and communitas: Victor Turner, The Ritual Process: Structure and Anti-Structure (1969). The liminal phase as dissolution of social structure; communitas as the ego-less bonds formed in shared liminality.

BDNF in physical hardship: see Chapter 5 references. Neuroplasticity triggered by sustained physical stress; BDNF as the neurochemical mechanism.

Prefrontal cortex fatigue in endurance: multiple sources, including studies on the degradation of decision-making under sustained physical and cognitive load.

Song reference for Stage Four: 'The Rain' by Oran 'Juice' Jones (1986).

CHAPTER 9 - THE DESCENT: THE ARCHITECTURE OF YOUR ORDEAL

During muddy rain sections of endless woods in Moab, I came to see the ordeal and life as a series of movies we make. More on that later; for now, let's script yours.

Time to Make Your Movie

Figure 9.1: Time to Make Your Movie
The ordeal you design will be the story you tell yourself for the rest of your leadership life. Make it worth telling.

By choosing a vision quest, you are strengthening your core self-belief. By this, I mean reaching a settled, unshakeable knowing: I will be okay no matter what. I am capable of dealing with whatever comes my way. I will not reduce my shine nor compromise my integrity, no matter the conditions.

At completion, you will know what it means to become unfuckable with.

Far from being a selfish act, reaching this state makes you more available to help others. A leader with a tempered core provides a stable foundation for the people who lean on them. But you do not reach that state without what my mother would have called a 'severe kick-in'. You are carrying out biological engineering designed to force a system reboot. The core principle is simple: if the challenge does not scare you or push you toward confronting the child self, it is not a quest. It is a change of scenery.

> *Think of this as a great movie. One that people would pay to watch. It will be full of mess-ups, anguish, humor, love, failing, trying again, and overcoming setbacks. Through it, you will release your inner soul to be who it is meant to be.*

The clown makeup of a professional persona will run. People will have to take you or leave you, straight, no chaser.

The Biological Gauntlet

You do not reach a state of being unfuckable with by attending a weekend seminar in a climate-controlled hotel. Most people spend their lives decorating the rooms of the identity they already own. But to build an Inner Citadel, you have to break ground on your biology.

The challenge must be hard enough to cause ego collapse. It must include solitude, vast nature, and sustained effort sufficient to fatigue the prefrontal cortex and open the subconscious. This is not a metaphor for discomfort. It is a description of a specific neurological event that only sustained physical and psychological hardship can trigger.

The aMCC, the Anterior Midcingulate Cortex, is the hub for tenacity. It grows when you do things you do not want to do. In a section of the Moab, I had to force-feed myself to maintain enough caloric intake to keep moving. So that structure was undergoing a growth spurt. You are becoming hard-headed in a literal, biological sense. This is not mysticism. It is neural weightlifting.

The Selection Protocol

How do you choose your specific descent? Five rules.

Figure 9.2: The Selection Protocol
The rules that determine whether your chosen ordeal will do the work. Not every hard thing qualifies.

1 **The Incompetence Rule**
Identify the things you are already good at and avoid it entirely. If you are a skilled runner, a 50k is not a quest. Your quest must take place in a domain where you feel like a child self: vulnerable, clumsy, and entirely out of your depth.

2 **The Oh Shit Test**
If the magnitude of the commitment does not deflate your happy balloon and make you think, 'Oh shit,' you have not picked a challenge hard enough to break through to the person you are meant to be.

3 **The Landscape of Scale**
Choose a place where the environment is indifferent to you: mountains, ocean, or deep forest. It must be large enough that your personal anxieties feel microscopic. This quiets the Default Mode Network, the part of the brain responsible for the anxious inner chatter that fills every quiet moment at your desk.

4 **Solo Digital Amputation**
You must be unreachable. At Moab, I ran alone, no pace runner to protect me. If your brain knows that rescue is a tap away, it never truly enters the ordeal state. The severance must be complete.

5 **The Duration Requirement**
It must last long enough to fatigue the prefrontal cortex. I recommend at least three days, based on personal experience. The first day breaks you in. The second day breaks you up. On the third day, you become fully broken and can be rebuilt. Moab was four days. By the fourth, I had been rebuilt. Physically, I had begun to deteriorate. Mentally, I was a fortress.

Choose What Breaks You, Not What Flatters You

When I chose Moab, I chose heat and altitude intentionally, because I go to pieces in both.

I am a real-life Mr. Bean in the outdoors. I cannot carry a knife without managing to cut myself. My navigation is so unreliable that when I think a direction is correct, I choose the opposite, because I know I am probably wrong. Heat and altitude shut me down to the point where I stop moving, panic, and give up. I had failed repeatedly in those conditions and knew that my current mental fortitude would not be adequate for what Moab required. I had to find a way to be significantly better.

A perfectly selected vision quest.

If you only quest in areas where you are already competent, you are not building a Citadel. You are redecorating a room you already own. The selection has to be made from the domain where you are most likely to fail, because that is where the growth lives.

Training for the Ordeal

Choose something that requires months of preparation: physical training, research, and a pre-set plan for how you will cope when you want to quit, because you will want to quit.

For Moab, I ran for months using mantras from Jim Murphy's book Inner Excellence: mantras of courage, wisdom, and patience, rehearsed daily so they would be available when the hard moments arrived. I had arrived at a truth that took time to find: I would not quit, no matter what. Not as a wish. Not as strong words. Not as a belief. As a 100% commitment, with no optionality built in. Quitting was not a choice.

If you feel fear at the thought of a vision quest, good. Fear will be a constant companion out there. The work is learning to act on it rather than letting it stop you.

The Menu

Below are eleven vision quests. Read down the list slowly. The one that makes your stomach turn is probably yours.

Figure 9.3: The Vision Quest Menu
A list of potential challenges you can consider.

Quest	The Hard Element
The Dry-Stone Wall	Build 20 feet of wall in a remote location by hand over 4 days.
The Weaver's Silence	Spin wool and weave a garment over 4 days in total silence.
The Solo Fast	4 days in a fixed outdoor location with only water. No food, no company, no escape.
The No-Clock Solo	4 days in the wild with no electronics and no way to measure time.
The Monk's Bell	Perform a physical manual task every 60 minutes for 72 consecutive hours.
The High-Altitude Navigation	Traverse a 10,000ft range using only a paper map. No GPS.
The Primitive Bivouac	48 hours in the forest or moorland with no modern survival gear.
The Animal Tracking Pursuit	Follow a specific animal's trail for 3 days, sleeping where you stop.
The Winter Debris Bivouac	Survive sub-freezing nights in a debris shelter you build yourself.
The Celestial Navigation Trek	Navigate 40 miles using only stars and the sun. No instruments.
The Canoe Build and Launch	Hollow a dugout canoe and navigate it 10 miles. Start with a log.

None of these is right or wrong. And there are many others you can consider. The question is not which one looks impressive. The question is which one genuinely excites & frightens you.

Voices from the Other Side

Before you commit, read below from fellow vision quest survivors:

> *"I groveled in my little circle. But that was the point. I did what I set out to do, and my heart is more relaxed than I have ever known."*
> Wilderness Quest Participant

> *"That vision quest saved my life. When I returned, I found a new sense of belonging, a clarity of who I am and who I am not."*
> Eddy Robinson, Indigenous Quester

Steven Foster and Meredith Little, pioneers of the modern wilderness rite of passage, recorded something that stayed with me:

> *"Most people report that fasting was not the difficult part"* They go on to say how the psyche easts all our thoughts and emotions instead. Further that *"Fasting erases the boundary between the self and nature."* This is profoundly true as I also experienced feeling complete and at one with my environment. They also beautifully explain the enrichment feeling: *"The person who returns from a wilderness fast may have a hungry body, but the soul, the mind, and the spirit have been fed."*
> Steven Foster and Meredith Little, Wilderness Resources

The Declaration of Severance

Put this book down. Right now.

Go and find a mirror. Take your time. Look hard. Quieten your breath.

Say: I am in.

Then commit to a vision quest. Do not overthink it. Book the travel. Register for the event. Tell your spouse. Feel the Oh Shit sensation.

When you do that, your brain has already begun to thicken. Your movie has started.

The quest begins the moment the commitment becomes irre-

versible.

See you in the woods.

Further Resources & References

Jim Murphy, Inner Excellence. Mindset training and mantras of courage and patience for sustained high-friction environments.

Steven Foster and Meredith Little, School of Lost Borders. Pioneers of modern wilderness rites of passage. The three-stage structure of Severance, Threshold, and Incorporation.

David Goggins, Can't Hurt Me. The physical and mental necessity of voluntary hardship for 'callousing the mind' and building resilience.

Eddy Robinson, When I Was 18, I Went on a Vision Quest [News article]. First-person account of the traditional Indigenous quest as a tool for identity, belonging, and biological recalibration.

John P. Milton, Way of Nature. Psychological and restorative effects of deep, sustained solitude and immersion in nature on the human nervous system.

Arnold van Gennep, The Rites of Passage. The foundational anthropological text codifying the three stages of transformation: Separation, Transition, and Incorporation.

Dr. Andrew Huberman (Huberman Lab), The Science of Tenacity. Biological proof that the aMCC physically thickens under voluntary hardship.

Victor Turner, The Ritual Process. The liminal state is a temporary shedding of status that enables psychological breakthrough.

Dacher Keltner, Awe: The New Science of Everyday Wonder. How vast landscapes deactivate the Default Mode Network and reduce the ego's grip.

Mircea Eliade, Rites and Symbols of Initiation. The ordeal, as a symbolic death, required the shedding of the outdated persona.

Joe Del Conte, Moab 240 Race Report. Mental and physical thresholds reached during extreme endurance are used as a case study for the method.

Minda Zetlin, Why I Went on a Vision Quest. Contemporary executive perspective on self-confrontation and clarity in the wilderness.

CHAPTER 10 - THE REVELATION: WHEN THE NOISE FALLS AWAY

At somewhere around mile 140, something broke.
Not my will. The dam that had been holding back a lifetime of accumulated tension.

I found myself sobbing uncontrollably in the middle of the desert. There was no specific emotional trigger, no singular thought of profound grief or overwhelming self-pity. My body was simply, violently weeping. It happened multiple times over the next two days.

The Third Day

For years, I had built a fortress of composure to navigate the modern world. We all do. We absorb the micro-traumas of back-to-back meetings, the crushing weight of executive decisions, and the incessant, buzzing anxiety of the digital age, and we lock it away in our tissues. We suppress the pressure because society and our own ego demand a stoic face. We are taught that holding it together is a sign of strength.

But out there, stripped to the studs by extreme exhaustion, the social mask had completely dissolved. I was no longer an executive or a strategist. I was just an animal in the dirt. And my body was finally doing exactly what a wild animal does when it survives a brush with death.

In the wild, when an antelope escapes a cheetah, it does not casually trot back to the herd to graze. It stands paralyzed for a moment, and then its entire body goes into a violent, involuntary tremor. It physically shakes off the event. That neurogenic shaking is a biological reset button: a kinetic purge that burns off the massive, toxic cocktail of adrenaline and cortisol generated during a fight-or-flight response. The physical trembling signals to the nervous system that the threat has passed, allowing the animal to return to rest and digest safely.

> *Humans are one of the only species arrogant enough to try to think our way out of this physical debt. We suppress the shake. We swallow the tears. We let the ghost of the hunt settle into our bones, where it crystallizes into chronic anxiety, insomnia, and burnout.*

My uncontrollable sobbing on the trail was my body's neurogenic shake. The ordeal of 240 miles had driven me into such profound physical depletion that my brain no longer had the calories to maintain the armor. The crying was the visceral, mechanical discharge of not just the agony of the previous 140 miles, but the invisible ultras I had been running in the boardroom for decades.

When the tears finally stopped, the shift was undeniable. I did not feel weak or defeated. I felt hollowed out, clean, and fundamentally reset. The survival debt was paid. For the first time in years, the noise was gone. Calmed, forged, a silverback again.

The Ego Collapse: Hallucinations in the Desert

With the emotional backlog cleared, the boundaries of perception began to fold.

By the middle of day two, the hallucinations started, and they only grew more vivid as time passed. They were entirely real: the boundary between the dream world and the physical world dissolved completely. My favorite was a group of lions playing cards, one of them looking directly at me, cigarette in hand, casually flicking its ash. There were endless animals, people building structures, objects of everyday objects that seemed one hundred percent physically present but were nothing more than mirages.

This is what happens when the executive controller in the brain finally shuts down. The rigid, algorithmic grip lets go, and what remains is entirely unencumbered.

Into the second night the weather broke, a clear sky allowed the darkness and stars to set wonderment into my psyche. I spent a painfree ten hours running effortlessly and thinking deeply, and I arrived at something I had not been able to articulate to myself before. Every problem I had decided existed, every irritant, from soaked feet to hiring errors, was a story I had concocted, made better or worse by the director's cut I applied to it. Not some of them. All of them.

Only hire happy ending writers to script your movie

The Revelation: Mile 200

The final clarity arrived on day three into four. After waking at Geyser Pass, mile 200, my brain, utterly deprived of comfort, brought the quest's core revelation into sharp focus.

It sounds simple. It was not.

Clean running water is a luxury. Everything else is a mirage of wants, not needs.

Back home, water arrives without effort or attention. Endless and invisible. Out there, we ran out. Even with aid stations, the water was occasionally contaminated and caused me real problems. I had several hours of poor gut and weakness. Every decision I made, pace, distance, survival, had to revolve around water. Without it, nothing else matters. At all. There is no second category.

Our modern abundance has become entirely invisible to us. That understanding did not arrive as a thought. It arrived as a fact the body had always known and had simply never been given the conditions to say out loud.

That clarity became the seed for everything I did next.

> *It stripped away the final layers of professional complication. What remained was not a plan or a purpose statement. It was a direction, carved in, with no optionality attached.*

Your Quiet Signal

Your revelation will not be about clean water.

It will be the specific, uncomfortable truth hidden beneath your busy workweeks and digital fog. The thing your prefrontal cortex has been successfully suppressing for years, because it is inconvenient, because it would require a difficult conversation, because acting on it would mean giving something up.

The ordeal removes the suppression. Not gently.

It might arrive as the heavy knowledge that you are building a business you know is going the wrong way. The stark recognition that you are leading from fear and control rather than from conviction. The realization that you are with the wrong people, or doing the wrong work, and that you have been choosing the comfort of the cage over the difficulty of the door.

Or it might arrive as relief. The sudden, profound recognition: I already have enough. I can stop chasing. Or as gratefulness, that desire to commit further to your mission with long-time colleagues and drive the communitas you seek.

> *A true revelation does not announce itself with fireworks. It arrives with a gravitational pull. It is the Alidade needle of an Astrolabe, locating the sun so you can place your position and direction on this earth with confidence.*

The freedom from both known and unknown shackles is a gift I find hard to articulate. But it is one I wish upon anyone brave enough to pack up, leave the comfort trap, and walk out into the dirt to earn it.

Further Resources & References

Neurogenic tremoring as biological reset: Levine, P. (1997). Waking the Tiger: Healing Trauma. The mechanism by which involuntary physical trembling discharges accumulated fight-or-flight hormones, enabling the nervous system to return to a parasympathetic baseline.

HPA-axis suppression and emotional armor: van der Kolk, B. (2014). The Body Keeps the Score. The physiological storage of unresolved stress in tissue and the pathways by which somatic discharge enables resolution.

Prefrontal cortex fatigue and ego dissolution: see Chapter 8 references. Executive function degradation under sustained physical load, and the emergence of rawer cognitive modes as the executive controller loses dominance.

Moab hallucination footage: TikTok @glazeruns (2025). Instagram Reel @glazeruns (2025). First-person documentation of perceptual dissolution during the Moab 240 endurance event.

CHAPTER 11 - THE RETURN: THE HARDEST PART TO GET RIGHT

Immediately after the race finished, I could not walk. My feet had blown up like the Nutty Professor in the movie. As the ordeal adrenalin had left, my body had swelled. Arriving at the airport, I was transported on a cart to reach the exit. It was weirdly fun! The dirt washes off. The blisters heal. The swelling goes down. It took me four weeks to move normally again. I had survived the Descent, and for a brief window, felt invincible. The noise gone, the signal clear, my Inner Citadel standing firmer than ever.

But make no mistake: the true ordeal does not happen in the desert. It happens the moment you unlock your front door.

The Danger of Re-Absorption

On completion, you will have a clear sense of what to make of your life. Your purpose, how you wish to live in community with others, what work you want to do and why, and with whom. Also, a deeper respect & relationship with self and nature. Wonderful! But danger threatens this clarity; don't get complacent.

When I stepped off the trail and made it home to Florida, the physiological shift was immediate. The environment began broadcasting comfort before I had unpacked. The temperature was perfectly controlled. Clean water flowed effortlessly from the tap. My biology, inherently programmed for the law of least effort, immediately began trying to glue those epigenetic survival manuals back shut.

Comfort is an invisible drug, and the modern world is relentlessly determined to sedate you. The fridge keeps your food cold. Coffee is effortless. The showers run warm. The couch is deep. The dishes wash themselves. This cocoon has a cost, and it's paid in the currency of everything you just earned.

The mechanism is not subtle. The moment I opened my laptop to review marketing analytics for a portfolio company, the vacuum was filled. The Red Queen Effect instantly hijacks the prefrontal cortex: the panic of needing to run twice as fast just to stay in place. The profound clarity of the Quiet Signal you fought so hard to hear is easily drowned out by the High-Speed Drift of the inbox.

Without an anchor, the profound revelations of the trail become nothing more than a story you tell at a dinner party.

This is not a weakness. It is biology. The nervous system does not distinguish between the comfort of home and the comfort of before. It simply returns to its prior operating tempo, because that is what nervous systems do, which is precisely why the Return requires as much deliberate architecture as the Descent.

The Three Lintels

There is a critical triangle that sustains the Inner Citadel on return. Lose any side of it, and the structure begins to hollow out. These are your Citadel lintels.

Figure 11.1: The Three Lintels of the Inner Citadel
Remove any one of them, and the structure does not hold.

	Lintel	Function
I	**Connection to Nature**	The body's baseline. Without it, the nervous system runs on abstraction, and the aMCC softens.
II	**Mind Integrated with Body**	The engine of self-respect. Built in the ordeal and maintained by daily friction.
III	**Leadership in Service of Community**	The output of the other two. Hollow without them. Sovereign with them.

These three sides are interdependent. The connection to nature is not an aesthetic preference. It is the body's calibration mechanism: without it, the nervous system loses its reference point for reality, and the aMCC begins to soften. The integration of mind and body is what the ordeal built. It is not a state you arrive at. It is a practice you maintain through daily friction, physical effort, and the regular return to discomfort. Leadership in the service of community is the output of the other two. Hollow without them. Sovereign with them.

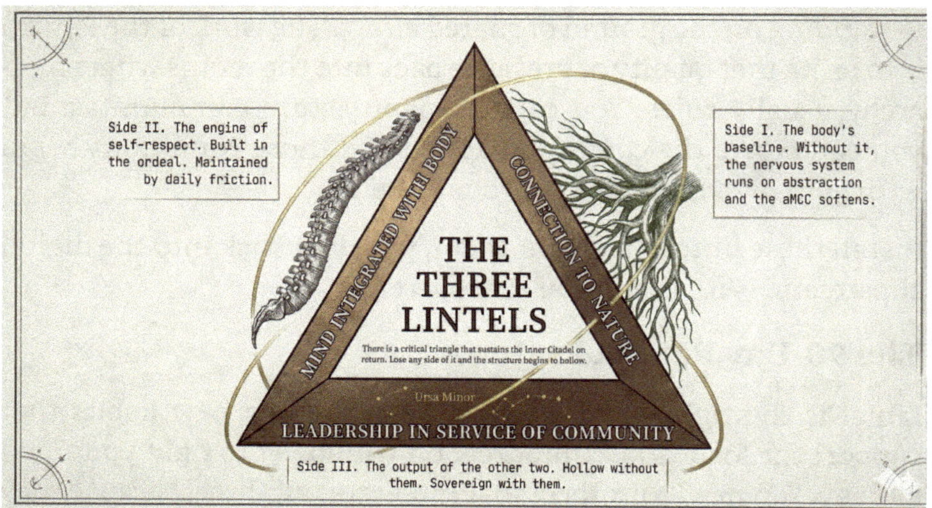

Figure 11.2: The Three Lintels Working Together
Separately, they are disciplines. Together, they are a life that does not require escape.

Artificial separation from the ground and from sunlight withers us. When the body stops solving real physical problems, the mind fills the gap with abstraction. We become slot machine junkies: perpetually stimulated, perpetually unsatisfied, unable to put the device down long enough to recognize the person standing next to us as fully human.

The reversal is specific, not philosophical.

You take the sun's warming of your smile back into the meeting. A mountain builds your heart and confidence for the presentation. A fence you build with your hands mends your mind as much as the boundary it creates.

When nature, body, and mind work together, something becomes available that no factory can manufacture and no wellness program can replicate. The people around you feel it. They lean in rather than disengage. They follow rather than comply.

A vision quest gives you the gratitude for your personal and professional network & the enlightenment of communitas: that rare state where the artificial walls of status dissolve because everyone is standing on the ground of shared effort. The work of the Return is to bring that quality of presence back into the rooms where hierarchy usually rules. You cannot manufacture communitas. But you can create the conditions for it, and those conditions begin with your own grounded nervous system.

Install these lintels. Without them, you drift back into the digital slipstream. With them, you are sovereign.

The 90-Day Return Protocol

Lintel is the right word. You need to establish new habits that support the load. You cannot rely on willpower to fight your own biology. You need a protocol that integrates all three, because they are not three independent habits. They are a structure, and structures are built from the ground up.

Lintel I holds the biological ground. Lintel II maintains the instrument (your body and mind). Lintel III is what the instrument is for. You cannot shortcut the sequence any more than you can build a roof before the walls.

Phase 1: Days 1–30, All Lintels Set

Purpose: Reset the biological baseline. Return the nervous system to its reference point for what is real. Without this, everything built in Stage 2 and 3 is constructed on abstraction.

The Hard Start. Immediate physical discomfort, first thing: cold shower, yoga, 5:30 am outdoor movement - walk, bike, or run, preferably in nature. Something that spikes the aMCC before the Red Queen starts running. This is not punishment. It is a daily statement of intent. Connecting will to movement.

The Natural Hour. No email/messaging for the first 60 minutes of each day's start. Meditate, run, plan, or read in a nature-filled location. If early meetings are unavoidable, take them on a walk through a natural space (Cities have them, too). Move your task list to paper and identify the three things that will actually move the dial. Deep thought on long-term success.

The Communitas Meeting. Move one high-stakes meeting per week from the office or video call to a trail or another nature-filled walk. The physical environment changes the quality of the conversation. You are not just changing the location. You are changing the biological state that both people bring to it. Do this deliberately and watch what changes.

If you miss a day, you do what you did to finish your quest, shrug it off, and go again. Vision questors have not quit left in them.

Phase 2: Days 31–60, Your Mind Body Skills Developed

Purpose: Maintain what the ordeal built. The aMCC grows under voluntary effort and softens without it. These practices are the daily friction that keeps the instrument sharp.

The Building Task. A physical craft or build project that requires body and mind to coordinate in solving a real problem together. Build something. Fix something. Make something with your hands. The material is irrelevant. The friction is the point. Doing this with and for others is even better, as it also places you in service.

Communication Batching. Lump all reading of email and messaging into fixed windows. AI tools make this easier. Track how many times you checked each day and work toward five or fewer. The goal is not effectiveness. The goal is to demonstrate to your nervous system that you are in charge of it, not the other way around. For speed and urgency, colleagues can call you. There is no excuse.

Phase 3: Days 61–90, Now Develop Your Team

Purpose: Convert the personal work of Phases 1 and 2 into an outward stance. This is the strength forming the other two lintels give you. It cannot be performed authentically before they are established. Now it can.

Level Up Projects. You have been back for 60 days, and you have practiced control. Now share your Code of Return with your team. State clearly how you will work, what you care deeply about, and invite them in to support. This is not a preference. It is a structural uplifting. State it once, calmly, and hold it. A culture of shared standards & communitas 'hard' projects that motivate and excite can begin.

The Ordeal Test. A 24-hour small-group quest with no technology, minimal gear, and high physical output. The purpose is to verify that your noise floor has held. If it has, you will feel the difference immediately on return. If it has not, you now know.

The vision quest does not give you a new identity. It strips away the borrowed one.

What you protect in the 90 days after is the self that was always underneath: the one that existed before the inbox, before the status, before the years of professional performance. The one that knows, without needing to be told, what actually matters.

The Inner Citadel is not built in the wilderness. It is only discovered there. The building happens here, in ordinary life, one non-negotiable at a time.

PART IV - THE EMBODIED LEADER

CHAPTER 12 - BUILDING A LIFE THAT DOESN'T REQUIRE ESCAPE

I had just covered 240 miles of rock, heat, altitude, and sleep deprivation. I had sobbed in the desert. I had hallucinated lions. I had arrived at the cellular understanding that clean water is wealth, and everything else is preference. I had earned something real.

Not a qualification. Not a framework. A self. The one that existed before the inbox, before the years of professional performance, before the slow abrasion of compromise had worn the instrument down to something I barely recognized. My mother had it. The silverback has it. The matriarch elephant, who walks to the front when the predator arrives, has it. The capacity to be fiercely protective of those in your care, not from anxiety, but from genuine strength. For the first time in two years, I was genuinely excited to do difficult work, to stand at the front of hard challenges, and to help the people around me win.

And within seventy-two hours, the comfort of my own home was doing its quiet work to take it back.

We are a species built to survive hardship. We have spent a century engineering hardship out of our lives. The result is not contentment. The result is drift.

The next three chapters are about refusing that drift. Not dramatically. Not by quitting your job or moving to the mountains. By understanding, precisely and practically, what the embodied leader does in the room, every day, against the full weight of a world designed to sedate them.

> *To live a life choosing Hard is not about being a martyr or a monk. It is about ensuring that the person who endured the ordeal does not become a fleeting ghost, but a permanent resident of your character.*

Living Differently, Not Dramatically

Returning from a vision quest does not mean quitting your job to live in a cave.

I am still a venture builder. I still do much of what I did before. But the how has changed in ways that are not negotiable.

I still choose the silverback approach (or Savanna Elephant Matriarch for female leaders), of embodied leadership. That is to enable and protect the teams in my care so they can do their work and grow. Now, though, with a harder stare at those in our way, and more love for those battling hard to achieve their own missions.

Living differently means you stop shrinking your identity to fit into rooms that demand your compromise. You hold your boundaries calmly amidst the noise. You operate with a biological noise floor so high that the daily friction of business barely registers. You have paid the price for the ticket to become unfuckable with. You simply refuse to hand that power back.

> *The quest does not change what you do. It changes what you will and will not tolerate while doing it.*

For me, integration means working with my hands in the physical world: building things, learning crafts I am bad at, creating structures and services that require the body and mind to work together. So I have designed a device-free leadership accelerator for founders, funders, and operators. The goal is to tether leadership teams to the communitas we experience in the wild when accomplishing hard things together back at the office. You need to build your team a dedicated practice to keep your collective edge sharp when the corporate world tries to soften you. When I stepped out of the Utah desert and back into the hum of work and normal life, the greatest threat was not behind me. It was waiting at home.

The Fallacy of the Escape

We have built a professional culture on a cycle of binge and purge. Most of us grind ourselves to a pulp for fifty weeks a year, then spend two weeks on holiday trying to recover a self that the other fifty weeks systematically dismantled. We imagine that a change of scenery can repair a soul worn down by years of going the wrong way. It cannot.

This is a failure of architecture. Meaning is not something you find on a beach in Portugal. It is the structure you inhabit every day. You do not need a holiday. You need a foundation that does not crumble under the first sign of pressure.

> *If your daily life is a prison of convenience, no vacation will set you free.*

Choosing Hard

The Anterior Midcingulate Cortex is the anatomical seat of human tenacity. It grows when you do things you do not want to do. It shrinks when the demands of life are removed. It is a use-it-or-lose-it organ, and the modern comfort economy is working against it every hour.

I have watched successful people function far below their potential because they have mistaken comfort for achievement. They stopped learning. They stopped growing. They stopped confronting the limits of their own resolve. The capacity that made them exceptional was quietly dissolving, and the comfort was so complete they could not feel it happening.

> *Ease is a slow-acting toxin. The symptoms take years to appear, and by then, they are easy to blame on something else.*

The Digital Moat

The digital world is designed to consume every millisecond of your attention. It is not neutral infrastructure. It is an environment built to keep you in a state of low-grade vigilance, vaguely unsatisfied, perpetually stimulated, and never quite present.

You cannot lead others fully, fairly, and with the care you and they would wish if you are a fugitive from your own silence. The Severance practiced in the quest is not a technique for the wilderness. It is a discipline for ordinary life: a commitment to regular periods of digital darkness that protect the signal you fought so hard to find.

The Enduring Self

Adopting to install the lintels, choosing hard every day, and having a digital moat are not habits. They are the materials of your Inner Citadel. Each one is a daily act, a refusal to let what the ordeal built quietly erode under the weight of convenience.

Life is bumpy. It is an endless losing and regaining of one's balance. The goal is not a state of permanent clarity, untouched by difficulty. The goal is a self that can meet difficulty without being consumed by it.

You were not built for a life of sedation. You were built for challenge, for effort, and for the quiet dignity of a life that has meaning. The ingredients are there. You are the only one who can put them together into the unique pattern that will be your life.

Let it be a life that hits its target.

CHAPTER 13 - HOW YOU SHOW UP

The 90-day protocol gave you the architecture. Chapter 12 gave you the practices. What neither can give you is the decision to actually inhabit what you built.

Most leaders who return from an ordeal manage the experience. They carry it carefully, like something fragile, referencing it in conversation, protecting it from the friction of ordinary life. Managing it is not the same as living from it. The Inner Citadel is not a memory you tend. It is a place you occupy.

You can now stop managing your personality and start occupying it.

The Urgent

My wife kindly describes my impatience as "high urgency." She is being generous. In the past, impatience was not a leadership quality. It was organized chaos for those who worked for me. I was in High-Speed Drift: moving fast, burning out the tires, covering anxiety with velocity.

The science of this is unambiguous. When you lead from impatience, you are operating from your sympathetic nervous system. Your body is flooded with cortisol and adrenaline. This is efficient for escaping a predator. It is catastrophic for strategic thinking. Cortisol inhibits the prefrontal cortex: the part of your brain responsible for complex decision-making, impulse control, and empathy.

> *When you are operating from anxiety, you are literally making yourself stupider. And taking your team with you.*

I had to learn this the hard way on the mud-caked cliffs of the Moab trails. Urgency differs from impatience and is highly valuable at the right time, especially in startups, where speed is a core competence. And out there, it was not useful. It was a liability. A rushed step meant a fall. A panicked decision meant getting lost in freezing rain at altitude. I implemented mantras specifically focused on patience: slow the physical movement, slow the breath, think clearly, re-engage the prefrontal cortex.

That is the Silverback energy. Not aggression. Not dominance. A calm, grounded presence that observes the environment completely before acting with precision. The silverback does not rush. It does not need to. Its authority is not in its speed. It is in its stillness.

> **The Three-Second Pause**
> When a crisis hits, do not react instantly. Take three seconds before speaking. Count them. This silence signals to everyone in the room that the situation is under control.
> **Why it works:** *Interrupts the sympathetic hijack. Gives the prefrontal cortex time to re-engage. The silence is read by your team as authority, not hesitation.*

> **Box Breathing**
> 4 seconds in, 4 hold, 4 out, 4 hold. You can do this in a meeting without anyone knowing. Practice it before high-stakes conversations until it is automatic.
> **Why it works:** *Physically forces the nervous system out of fight-or-flight and back into lead-and-decide. This is not a relaxation technique. It is a performance tool.*

The Interoceptive Leader

Endurance running at the level of the Moab 240 forces a very specific skill: distinguishing between productive pain and injury pain. Get this wrong, and you either quit too early or destroy something that takes months to repair. The difference between the two is not in the pain itself. It is in learning to read what your body is actually telling you, accurately, in real time, under duress.

This is interoception: the ability to sense and interpret the internal state of your own body. It is processed in the Insula, a structure that integrates bodily sensations with emotional processing. High-performing leaders have superior interoceptive awareness. They can sense when a deal is off before the data confirms it. They notice when a team member is holding something back before it surfaces in a meeting. Not because they are psychic. Because they are tuned to the subtle physiological shifts in their own bodies, and those shifts are reliable signals.

The ordeal trains this. Four days in the desert, with no distractions, no devices, no escape from your own physical state, and you develop a relationship with your body's signals that a thousand mindfulness apps could not produce.

The 60-Second Scan
Before any high-stakes meeting, take one minute to scan your body from feet to shoulders. Are your shoulders tight? Is your breath shallow? Is your jaw set? Do not evaluate what you find. Simply register it.
Why it works: *Creates a pre-meeting baseline. What you notice is information. What you ignore accumulates.*

Label the Sensation
Do not say 'I am stressed.' Say: 'I feel a tightness in my chest.' The precision is the practice. Vague emotional labeling keeps you in the amygdala—specific somatic labeling shifts neural activity to the prefrontal cortex.
Why it works: *The act of precise labeling is itself a regulation tool. It does not require that you resolve the feeling. It requires that you name it accurately.*

The War on Entropy

In basic physics, energy spreads out. Without active input to maintain order, systems decay into chaos. In business, entropy looks like meeting bloat, forty-person Slack channels, and the institutional need to be seen to be busy.

Every minor decision, what to wear, which email to answer first, how to word a message, depletes your cognitive budget. By the time you reach the strategic decisions that actually move the needle, you are running on fumes. This is not a time management problem. It is a biology problem. And it has a structural solution.

Commander's Intent

At our Venture Builder, we do not give step-by-step instructions. We define the End State: what does success look like, and the inputs: what information and resources should be sourced? Once the team understands the intent, they make the micro-decisions on the 'how to do it' themselves. Your cognitive energy is reserved for the twenty percent of decisions that actually matter.

Why it works: *Distributing decision-making to the level where information is richest means the organization moves at the speed of the problem. Protects the leader's prefrontal cortex for strategic work.*

The No-Low Rule

If a task is low-impact and low-leverage, it should not reach your desk. If it does, your system has failed. Build the filter, not the habit of processing what the filter should have caught.

Why it works: *Every low-leverage item you personally handle is a training signal to your team that you are available for low-leverage items. Stop training for that. In a world of AI, they should be able to become self-sufficient on all but the most complex or high-priority tasks.*

The Stewardship of Calm

You are the thermostat of your organization. If you walk into a meeting wired and anxious, you are not just performing badly. You are triggering a survival response in the people around you that shuts down their capacity for creative and strategic thinking.

This is not a soft observation. It is a neurological one. Through mirror neurons, your team physically mirrors your physiological state. Your cortisol becomes their cortisol. Your calm becomes their calm. The quality of their thinking is, to a measurable degree, downstream of the state you bring into the room.

> *Calmness is not a personality trait. It is a leadership practice. And its absence is an ethical failure.*

The ordeal is, among other things, a training ground for this. Four days in which urgency is useless teach the nervous system that stillness is not passivity. It is the precondition for precision. You bring that back into the business not as a technique but as a state you have earned.

Designing the Cadence

Most executives are digital drifters: their calendars dictated by others' priorities, their days assembled by default rather than by design. At our ventures, we call this designing 'the cadence'. It is not a time management framework. It is a declaration of what you are protecting and why.

Deep Work Blocks *Strategic 'doing work' alone and with teams*	Protects the flow state and neuroplasticity that the ordeal reactivated. The prefrontal cortex requires uninterrupted time to do its best work. Meetings that fracture the morning are not a scheduling inconvenience. Meetings that solve and build solutions together are gold.
Asynchronous First *If it can be a document or a recording, it is not a meeting.*	Reduces context-switching and the cortisol spikes that accompany it. Every unnecessary meeting is a request that someone else pay the cost of your communication preference.
The Daily Stand-Up *15-minute sessions. One question: what is blocked, and who is moving it?*	Uses the aMCC's tenacity function. Short, high-friction, outcome-focused. The brevity is not a courtesy. It is the practice. Stopping entropy and keeping teams on track.

By refusing to let others design your communication, you protect the clarity found in the Descent. You shift from a reactive manager to an embodied leader. You stop telling people what to do and start providing a stable, high-clarity environment where they can do their best work.

> *The silverback does not manage the group's anxiety. It simply does not contribute to it.*

Further Resources & References

Cortisol and prefrontal cortex inhibition: Arnsten, A.F.T. (2009). Stress signaling pathways that impair prefrontal cortex structure and function. Nature Reviews Neuroscience.

Interoception and the Insula: Craig, A.D. (2009). How do you feel: now? The anterior insula and human awareness. Nature Reviews Neuroscience. Superior interoceptive awareness correlates with decision-making quality under uncertainty.

Mirror neurons and co-regulation: Iacoboni, M. (2009). Imitation, empathy, and mirror neurons. Annual Review of Psychology. The physiological state of a leader is literally transmitted to team members through neural mirroring mechanisms.

Decision fatigue and cognitive budget: Baumeister, R.F. et al. (1998). Ego depletion: Is the active self a limited resource? Journal of Personality and Social Psychology.

Commander's Intent: Moltke the Elder, Prussian military doctrine, 19th century. Operationalized in modern leadership contexts by Marquet, L.D. (2012). Turn the Ship Around.

Flow state and deep work: Newport, C. (2016). Deep Work. The neurological conditions for flow state require sustained, uninterrupted focus: conditions that meeting-fragmented schedules structurally prevent.

CHAPTER 14 - THE FUTURE OF YOUR LEADERSHIP

We are standing at a Great Divergence in leadership. Look around you. Two paths are forming. On one side stands the Abstract Leader: managing as a 'brain in a box'. Head in a dashboard, communicating via algorithm, making decisions from data stripped of human context, and moving fast. Scorching the earth and not noticing. This is the path of least resistance, and it leads to a hollow kind of authority that the people underneath it can feel immediately, even when they cannot name it. They are simply widgets, interchangeable with AI-agents, of no consequence.

On the other side stands the Embodied Leader: the Silverback or Elephant Matriarch, who has survived the Descent and returned with a nervous system capable of holding the weight of a hyperconnected world. Not because they have more information. Because they have more self.

> *As digital connectivity increases, the value of raw information is plummeting toward zero. When everyone has access to the same machines, the same data, and the same algorithms,*

> *your competitive advantage is no longer what you know. It is who you are when the pressure is on.*

Technology Is Not a Tool. It Is an Environment.

We must face a hard truth: technology is not neutral infrastructure. It is an environment, and for most leaders, a hostile one. In our current hyper-connected state, we are suffering from chronic activation of the stress response due to the constant, unpredictable demands of digital life. When you are always reachable, your brain never exits the state of low-grade vigilance. You are biologically incapable of deep work or strategic foresight. You are leading from a state of biological poverty.

Robert Sapolsky's research on chronic stress demonstrates that sustained activation of the stress response blunts the brain's capacity for pleasure in ordinary things and impairs the prefrontal cortex's ability to inhibit impulsive behavior. The more connected you are, the more likely you are to make reactive, low-clarity decisions. You are not controlling the technology. The technology's manufactured urgency is controlling your biology.

The leaders who will navigate the next decade are not the ones with the best tools. They are the ones whose nervous systems have not been colonized by those tools.

The Return of Biological Signaling

In a world of automated responses and synthetic content, what cannot be faked is presence. When you walk into a room after a vision quest, you carry something no algorithm can replicate. Your nervous system is genuinely regulated. Your attention is genuinely available. The people in the room feel it before you speak.

Dr. Stephen Porges' Polyvagal Theory explains the mechanism. Our nervous systems are continuously scanning the environment for signals of safety or threat. A leader who is anxious and abstract sends a threat signal, pushing the team into a defensive state and reducing their collective capacity for creative and strategic thought. A grounded leader sends a safety signal that unlocks what the team is actually capable of. The quality of the thinking in your organization is downstream of the state you bring into the room.

> *You cannot buy this signal. You cannot perform it. You can only earn it.*

The Ethics of the Silverback Approach

Being an Embodied Leader is not an exercise in dominance. In nature, the silverback's primary role is to provide a canopy of safety. As Simon Sinek observes in Leaders Eat Last, the alpha gets first choice of food, but pays for that privilege by being the one who runs toward the predator. In the digital world, the predators are burnout, algorithmic exploitation, and the slow erosion of meaning from work.

The Embodied Leader has an ethical obligation to manage their own nervous system so as not to infect the organization with secondhand anxiety. If you walk into a meeting wired from digital overwhelm, you are triggering your team's survival instincts. You are making it harder for the people who depend on you to think clearly. That is not a performance problem. It is a leadership failure.

Nassim Taleb's concept of skin in the game applies here with full force. If you have the rewards but do not share the risks, you are a parasite. The Silverback leads from the front. If the team is grinding, you are in the room. If the mud is deep, your boots are dirty.

The Only Unhackable Asset

Artificial intelligence can simulate intelligence. It cannot simulate will.

The will to endure is a biological property of the Anterior Midcingulate Cortex. It shrinks in the absence of challenge. It grows when you engage in voluntary hardship. As AI absorbs an increasing share of the cognitive load of management, the only thing left for the human leader is the load of will. The decisions no algorithm can make. The presence that no model can project. The trust no system can earn.

If you have not calloused your aMCC through daily choosing Hard, you will be replaced not because you lack intelligence, but because you lack the one thing the machine cannot replicate.

> *The final competitive advantage is not processing power. It is the capacity to endure, to be present, and to choose the difficult thing when the easy thing is available.*

The Guardian of the Human

My support crew at Moab was surprised by my pleasant nature and by my checking in on how they were, as they had been warned that runners are stressed, have little or no sleep, and can take it out on them. The Silverback leader acts as a firewall between the machine and the human. You protect the conditions under which people do their best work. In an economy increasingly built on automation, the temptation is to manage people as resources to be optimized. You value the hard work of a human over the easy output of a prompt, because one builds character and the other builds dependency. The world does not need more high-speed drifters. It needs leaders who have been somewhere real and returned.

> *"The things you learn in maturity aren't simple things, such as acquiring information and skills. You learn not to engage in self-destructive behavior. You find that the world loves talent, but pays off on character."*
>
> John W. Gardner, Personal Renewal (1990)

John Gardner spent his life studying what distinguishes leaders who grow from leaders who calcify. His answer was always the same: not talent, not intelligence, not even experience. Character.

The capacity to keep developing when development is uncomfortable. The willingness to be changed by what you encounter.

That is what the ordeal is. That is what every chapter of this book has been building toward. Not a technique. Not a framework. A life that keeps encountering real things and being shaped by them.

You have read this book. You know the argument.

You know what the drift costs. You know what the ordeal gives. You know that the Inner Citadel is not built in the wilderness: it is discovered there, and built here, in ordinary life, one non-negotiable at a time.

The only question that remains is the one you already know you have to answer.

When will you start?

Further Resources & References

Robert Sapolsky, Why Zebras Don't Get Ulcers (2004). Chronic stress and its suppression of prefrontal cortex function, including impulse control and complex decision-making.

Stephen Porges, The Polyvagal Theory (2011). The nervous system's continuous scanning for safety and threat cues, and how a leader's regulated state produces a measurable safety signal in those around them.

Simon Sinek, Leaders Eat Last (2014). The alpha's obligation to absorb risk and provide a canopy of safety for the group.

Nassim Taleb, Skin in the Game (2018). The ethical requirement that those who benefit from a system share its risks.

John W. Gardner, Personal Renewal (1990). Delivered as a speech to McKinsey and Company. The distinction between the accumulation of skills and the development of character as the true measure of maturity.

Andrew Huberman, Huberman Lab (2022). The Anterior Midcingulate Cortex as the seat of tenacity: use-dependent growth through voluntary hardship and micro-ordeals.

APPENDICES

APPENDIX A - THE BACK STORY

The people who matter, the life we lead, the stories still to write.

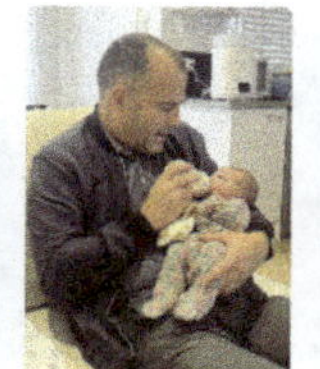

7

MOAB 240

MOAB 240

APPENDIX B - THE MANAGER'S FIELD GUIDE

Implementing the Hard in Your Team

The practices in this guide move a team from High-Speed Drift, reactive, anxious, and over-connected, to a state of Collective Coherence. As a manager, you are the architect of the team's environment. You cannot force resilience, but you can engineer the conditions in which it becomes the only logical outcome.

Each protocol below follows the same structure: the philosophy behind it, the science that supports it, and the tactical execution that makes it real.

1. Commander's Intent: The Silverback Protocol

The Philosophy
In high-entropy environments, detailed instructions are the first things to break down. The Silverback does not issue task lists. They define the End State and the Why, then step back. This is drawn from military doctrine and validated by Harvard leadership research: clarity of intent yields better outcomes than granularity of instruction.

The Science
Commander's Intent reduces cognitive load on the manager, pro-

tecting the aMCC from depletion, while requiring the team to engage their own problem-solving capacity. This is a micro-ordeal in itself: being trusted to navigate the mud of execution without a hand-hold.

Tactical Execution

- The End State Brief: Define success clearly before any project launches. Not what to do, but what done looks like: 'By Friday, the client must feel absolute confidence in our Q4 roadmap.'
- Freedom of Movement: Once intent is set, step back entirely. Allow the team to navigate execution. Resist the pull to intervene. Their resilience is built in the space you create.
- Weekly Intent Check: One question at the start of each week: 'Does everyone understand what winning looks like this week, and why it matters?' Not what they are doing. What they are trying to achieve.

2. Cadence Design: The War on Entropy

The Philosophy

Entropy in an organization manifests as meeting bloat and asynchronous noise. Left unmanaged, both consume the team's capacity for deep work until they are biologically incapable of excellence. Designing the communication cadence is not a scheduling exercise. It is a neurological one.

The Science

Research from the University of California, Irvine, shows it takes an average of 23 minutes to regain deep focus after a single interruption. A team that is always reachable is a team that never reaches its cognitive ceiling.

Tactical Execution

- The Hard Stand-Up: Daily, 15 minutes maximum, no chairs, in person where possible. Two questions only: What is the primary blocker? Who is moving it?
- Deep Work Sanctuaries: Designate protected blocks (e.g., Tuesday and Thursday mornings) where Slack and email are off-limits. Protect these against all non-critical encroachment.

- The Loom First Rule: If information can be conveyed via a recorded video or a written document, the meeting does not happen. Treat the team's attention budget as a finite, irreplaceable resource.

3. Collective Friction: Building the Team aMCC

The Philosophy

Resilience is not a personality trait. It is a biological muscle. The Anterior Midcingulate Cortex grows when individuals engage in activities they would rather avoid. A team that is never asked to be uncomfortable is a team that is quietly becoming fragile.

The Science

Dr. Andrew Huberman's work on the aMCC demonstrates use-dependent growth: the structure physically thickens under voluntary effort. A soft team is not a moral failure. It is a biological outcome of insufficient friction.

Tactical Execution

- Monthly Hard Challenge: Set a collective, non-work challenge once a month. A 5:30 am team hike. A group cold-plunge. A digital fast day. The activity matters less than the fact that it is chosen, shared, and difficult.
- Transparency of Struggle: Actively celebrate the hard parts of a project. Do not smooth over difficulty. Name it, frame it as evidence of grit, and mark it as something the team moved through together. This callouses the collective nervous system.
- Acknowledge the Grind: When a project is genuinely brutal, say so directly. 'This is hard, and we are doing it anyway' is more motivating than false positivity, and it is physiologically true.

4. Autonomic Co-Regulation: Managing the Room

The Philosophy

Your most powerful tool as a manager is your own nervous system. Through mirror neurons, your state of calm or anxiety is transmitted directly to the people around you. You are not just setting the tone. You are setting the biology.

The Science

Polyvagal Theory establishes that humans continuously scan their environment for signals of safety or threat. A regulated leader produces a safety signal that unlocks the team's prefrontal cortex for creative and strategic work. An anxious leader triggers a survival response that shuts it down.

Tactical Execution

- The Three-Second Pause: Before responding to a crisis or a heated question, pause for three seconds. This is not a weakness. It signals to the room that there is no immediate predator, and it gives your own prefrontal cortex time to re-engage.
- Low-Vibration Briefing: When delivering bad news, keep voice tonality low and steady. Ground yourself physically: feet flat, posture open. You are communicating safety through your body before you speak a word.
- Pre-Meeting Regulation: Take two minutes before any high-stakes meeting to regulate your own state. Slow exhale, physiological sigh, or a brief walk. You cannot co-regulate a team from a dysregulated state.

5. The Ethics of the Canopy

The Philosophy

The silverback's primary function is not authority. It is protection. As a manager, you have an ethical duty to absorb the noise from above, the board, the stakeholders, the digital fog, so that your team can do the hard work they were hired to do without being consumed by it.

The Science

Simon Sinek's Leaders Eat Last establishes the biological basis for this: the alpha's privilege is earned by being the one who runs toward the predator. The manager who passes organizational anxiety downward is not leading. They are amplifying the problem.

Tactical Execution

- Absorb, Don't Transmit: When senior pressure arrives, process it before passing it on. Translate urgency into a clear direction. Never deliver panic. Never forward anxiety without context.
- Digital Blackout Commitment: Schedule send of your messages to your team after 7 pm unless there is a genuine emergency or it's their preferred time. When you send messages outside the preagreed hours, you hinder their recovery. That recovery is not optional. It is the biological prerequisite for their performance tomorrow.
- Protect Deep Work: When someone in the team has a protected block, defend it against all non-critical interruptions, including your own. The canopy of safety includes the right to concentrate.

APPENDIX C - SCIENTIFIC FOUNDATIONS

The Biology of the Hard Leader

The transformation described in this book is not metaphorical. It is biological. This appendix provides the empirical scaffolding for the Hard philosophy: the specific mechanisms by which voluntary hardship rewires the nervous system, recalibrates the stress response, and builds the physiological foundations of embodied leadership.

For those who require the receipts: they are here.

1. The aMCC: The Seat of Will

Primary Research
Studies from the University of Pennsylvania and research summarised by Dr. Andrew Huberman identify the Anterior Midcingulate Cortex as a unique structure that integrates emotional, cognitive, and motor information. Unlike other brain regions that automate behavior, the aMCC is specifically activated by voluntary effort: doing things we would rather not do.

Key Finding
The aMCC is plastic. It grows in volume when individuals engage in micro-ordeals: cold exposure, endurance training, resisting im-

pulses. In states of High-Speed Drift where comfort is prioritized, this region physically shrinks. This is not a metaphor. It is a measurable structural change in brain tissue.

Leadership Application

A robust aMCC is the biological prerequisite for tenacity. Without it, the will to maintain direction under pressure is the first thing to fail during a market pivot, a personnel crisis, or a period of sustained uncertainty. Callousing the aMCC is the primary objective of the Hard Fix.

2. The HPA-Axis: The Cost of Digital Urgency

Primary Research

Robert Sapolsky (Stanford University) has extensively documented the impact of chronic stress on primate hierarchies. When a leader is constantly reactive to notifications and digital demands, the hypothalamus signals the pituitary gland to release ACTH, which triggers the adrenal glands to flood the system with cortisol.

Key Finding

High circulating cortisol has a direct inhibitory effect on the Prefrontal Cortex, the seat of strategic thinking, long-term planning, and impulse control. Chronic HPA activation keeps the brain anchored in the amygdala, the center for fear and reactivity. Leaders in this state make short-sighted, defensive decisions not because they lack intelligence, but because they are biologically unable to access their strategic brain.

Leadership Application

The vision quest resets the HPA-axis through acute voluntary stress (hormesis), followed by genuine recovery. This lowers the cortisol baseline, allowing the prefrontal cortex to re-engage. The business meeting feels less threatening because the nervous system has a new reference point for what threat actually means.

3. Heart Rate Variability and Polyvagal Theory

Primary Research

Dr. Stephen Porges' Polyvagal Theory describes the Social Engagement System: the mechanism by which humans continuously scan others for cues of safety or threat via the vagus nerve. This is not conscious. It is pre-cognitive, faster than thought, and it governs whether the people around you are in a state of creativity or survival.

Key Finding

Heart Rate Variability (HRV) is the primary metric for vagal tone. A high HRV indicates a flexible nervous system capable of moving fluidly between activation and recovery. Endurance training consistently produces higher HRV. Through mirror neurons, a leader with high HRV and a regulated vagus nerve co-regulates their team. By remaining calm, they lower cortisol levels in the room and unlock the team's prefrontal cortex.

Leadership Application

Leadership is a contact sport played through the nervous system. The quality of thinking in your organization is downstream of the biological state you bring into the room. No strategy document overrides a dysregulated nervous system in real time.

4. Epigenetics: The Hard Dividend

Primary Research

Emerging research in epigenetics suggests that physical stressors, including extreme endurance events and cold immersion, trigger the expression of sirtuins and heat shock proteins. These proteins assist in cellular repair and neuroprotection.

Key Finding

By integrating Hard protocols, the leader is cleaning their biological cache, resetting the stress-tolerance baseline so that ordinary workplace pressure no longer triggers a full survival response. The 'Digital Fog of a Tuesday afternoon' becomes measurably less threatening at the cellular level.

Leadership Application

The Hard Fix is not only a psychological shift. It produces lasting changes in gene expression that raise the baseline for stress tolerance, accelerate cellular repair, and extend the period of high cognitive performance across a career.

Summary: The Biology of the Hard Leader

Mechanism	Triggered By	Effect	Leadership ROI
aMCC Growth	Voluntary effort, micro-ordeals	Increased tenacity and will	Holds course under market chaos
HPA-Axis Reset	Hormesis: acute voluntary stress	Lower cortisol baseline	Prefrontal cortex re-engages
HRV Improvement	Endurance + recovery cycles	Higher vagal tone	Co-regulates the team's nervous system
Epigenetic Expression	Physical stress (cold, endurance)	Sirtuin and HSP activation	Cellular repair, stress tolerance baseline

APPENDIX D - ETHICAL GUIDELINES AND SAFETY

Including the Stair Protocol

The Hard Fix is a powerful instrument for neurological and physical transformation. Like any powerful instrument, it must be used with precision and respect. This appendix defines the necessary boundaries: the ethical obligations around cultural origin, the physical requirements for safe practice, and the principle of personal sovereignty that governs the entire philosophy.

1. Cultural Respect: Honoring the Origin

The term Vision Quest has deep, sacred roots in Indigenous cultures, particularly among the North American Plains peoples, including the Lakota and Anishinaabe, for whom the Hanbleceya (crying for a vision) was a spiritual rite of passage administered within a living community of knowledge and practice.

This book uses the term to describe a personal rite of transformation: a deliberate descent into voluntary hardship to gain clarity. That usage is distinct from those traditions, and the distinction matters.

Recognition: These traditions are not fitness trends or biohacks.

They are spiritual disciplines developed over generations and inseparable from the cultures that hold them.

Integrity: When designing your own version of a quest, do so with humility. The objective is personal transformation and a return to your own human baseline, not the appropriation of sacred ceremony. If you are drawn to an authentic Indigenous tradition, approach it through the proper channels of the communities that hold it.

2. Health Screening: The Biological Baseline

Before engaging in extreme endurance, prolonged fasting, or thermal stress, professional medical clearance is a non-negotiable requirement. This is not a liability disclaimer. It is practical wisdom.

Cardiovascular integrity: High-intensity Hard protocols place significant stress on the cardiovascular system. A history of hypertension, cardiac arrhythmia, or related conditions requires medical supervision before any protocol of significant physical intensity.

Nutritional safety: Fasting is a tool for mental clarity and metabolic reset, but it is contraindicated for those with metabolic disorders, a history of disordered eating, or who are pregnant or breastfeeding. Consult a clinician before any extended fast.

The Rule of Gradual Loading: A runner does not begin with a 240-mile race. Build physical and mental callousness incrementally. The first micro-ordeal is a cold shower. The first endurance challenge is a 10k. The body responds to progressive overload, not to sudden extremity.

3. Personal Sovereignty and Limits

The philosophy of the Silverback is built on personal sovereignty. The responsibility for applying these protocols rests entirely with the individual.

Liability: The author and publishers are not responsible for injuries or health complications resulting from practices described in this book. These materials are for informational purposes.

The Productive Friction Distinction: An embodied leader knows the difference between productive friction (discomfort that produces growth) and self-destruction (damage that produces nothing). If a protocol is causing sustained injury, chronic illness, or genuine burnout, it is no longer serving the mission of clarity. Stop. Recover. Recalibrate.

4. The Stair Protocol: The Inconvenience Rule

One of the most accessible micro-ordeals available to any leader, in any building, on any day, is the simple choice of stairs over an elevator. The cumulative biological dividend of this single daily decision is substantial.

> *The research is unambiguous: long-term stair climbing is associated with a 24% lower risk of death from any cause and a 39% lower risk of dying from cardiovascular disease.*

These figures come from large-scale studies published in the British Journal of Sports Medicine and the European Society of Cardiology. The mechanism is simple: brief, repeated elevations in heart rate produce cardiovascular adaptation over time. The aMCC activation from choosing the harder option, dozens of times a day, accumulates into a measurable structural effect.

The stair protocol is not a substitute for a vision quest. It is the daily maintenance of the disposition the quest installs: the habit of choosing friction when ease is available. It is, in miniature, exactly what this book is about.

APPENDIX E - THE HARD LEXICON

Core Terms and Definitions

A high-performance culture is built on shared language. The terms below are used with precision throughout this book. Understanding them as a system, not as isolated definitions, is part of the work.

The Hard Fix

The central philosophy of this book is that modern ease is a biological toxin and that the intentional reintroduction of friction, discomfort, and voluntary hardship is the mechanism by which leaders reclaim the nervous system, focus, and integrity that comfort erodes. Not punishment. A prescription.

High-Speed Drift

A state common among successful executives: moving fast, producing results, but operating in a reactive, anxious fog. Characterized by elevated cortisol, chronic context-switching, and a persistent sense of being busy but hollow despite professional achievement. The presenting condition this book treats.

The Descent

The first active stage of the Hard Fix. The deliberate move away from the comfort of ordinary life and into the ordeal: whether through a vision quest like the Moab 240, prolonged digital severance, or a structured physical challenge. The Descent is where the social mask begins to dissolve.

The Return

The most consequential stage of the transformation. Not the ordeal itself, but the integration of its lessons back into ordinary life. Without a structured Return, the clarity earned in the Descent remains a memory rather than a lived reality. The 90-day protocol exists to make the Return permanent.

The Inner Citadel

Borrowed from the Stoic tradition of Marcus Aurelius: the internal fortress of the mind that no external force can breach. Built through the accumulation of voluntary hardship, honest self-confrontation, and the daily maintenance of non-negotiable practices. Discovered in the wilderness. Built into ordinary life.

Silverback Leadership

The archetype of the Embodied Leader. Not dominant. Not aggressive. Grounded. The Silverback leads from calm, moves with high urgency and zero anxiety, and makes decisions from clarity rather than reactive pressure. The primary function is to provide a canopy of safety for those they lead.

Communitas

Victor Turner's term for the state of radical human equality that emerges during the liminal phase of transformation: the stripping away of status, title, and social role that occurs when people share extreme conditions. In communitas, CEOs and entry-level employees become simply human. This is not a soft concept. It is a neurological event.

Liminality

From the Latin limen: threshold. Anthropologist Victor Turner describes the in-between state of transformation. Neither what you were nor what you will become. The ordeal deliberately holds you in liminality because it is only in this state that deep identity change becomes possible.

aMCC (Anterior Midcingulate Cortex)

The physical seat of will and tenacity in the human brain. Grows in volume when individuals engage in voluntary effort: doing things they would rather avoid. Shrinks in states of chronic ease. The primary biological target of the Hard Fix. Not a metaphor. A measurable structure in brain tissue.

Autonomic Coherence

The physiological state in which the heart, brain, and nervous system operate in synchrony. Associated with high Heart Rate Variability and regulated vagal tone. A leader in a state of coherence co-regulates the people around them through mirror neurons: their calm becomes the team's calm.

Digital Severance

Not digital detox (a temporary purge) but a permanent restructuring of the relationship with technology: designating regular periods of total disconnection as a non-negotiable practice. The objective is to ensure the human remains sovereign and that the signal found in the ordeal is not immediately lost to the noise.

High-Speed Drift

See definition above. Distinguished from the Invisible Ultra (the unrelenting cognitive load of managing teams, families, and finances simultaneously, with no finish line and no recovery built in). The Invisible Ultra is a grind. High-Speed Drift is a choice made by increments.

Commander's Intent

A leadership protocol originating in military doctrine: define the End State and the Why with clarity, then delegate the How entirely. Reduces the manager's cognitive load while requiring the team to develop their own problem-solving capacity—a micro-ordeal for teams unaccustomed to autonomy.

The Original Stack

The environmental conditions our biology evolved for over 300,000 years: sunlight, temperature cycles, environmental porosity, fractal patterns, and varied terrain. Reconnecting with the Original Stack is the biological mechanism by which the Return sustains the gains of the Descent.

APPENDIX F - BIBLIOGRAPHY OF HEAVYWEIGHTS

The Evidence Base

The Hard Fix is only as strong as the evidence supporting it. What follows is the curated source base for the biological, anthropological, and strategic arguments made throughout this book. These are not passing citations. They are the intellectual architecture underneath the narrative.

1. Leadership, Strategy, and Adaptive Systems

These works redefine leadership not as a position of authority, but as a biological and systemic practice.

Heifetz, Ronald A. *Leadership Without Easy Answers*. Harvard University Press.

Core insight: *The distinction between technical problems (solvable with existing knowledge) and adaptive challenges (requiring a change in values, beliefs, or behavior). Embodied leadership is the primary instrument for adaptive challenges.*

Taleb, Nassim Nicholas. *Antifragile: Things That Gain from Disorder*. Random House.

Core insight: *Systems and leaders that are antifragile do not merely withstand shocks; they require them to grow. The philosophical foundation for seeking the Hard.*

Sinek, Simon. *Leaders Eat Last: Why Some Teams Pull Together and Others Don't.* Portfolio.

Core insight: *The biological basis of trust and the Circle of Safety. The framework for the Silverback's ethical duty to protect the team.*

Burnison, Gary. *The Leadership Journey.* Wiley / Korn Ferry Institute.

Core insight: *The importance of learning agility and the ability to navigate ambiguity, both honed through the Descent.*

Gardner, John W. *Personal Renewal (speech, 1990).*

Core insight: *The distinction between the accumulation of skills and the development of character as the true measure of maturity. Available at pbs.org/johngardner*

2. Neuroscience, Stress, and the aMCC

The leader's hardware is the brain. These sources detail the neurobiology of will, tenacity, and the cost of digital urgency.

Sapolsky, Robert M. *Why Zebras Don't Get Ulcers.* Stanford University / Holt Paperbacks.

Core insight: *The definitive account of how chronic stress (HPA-axis activation) ravages the primate body and inhibits the prefrontal cortex. Essential reading for any leader who confuses busyness with effectiveness.*

Huberman, Andrew. *The Huberman Lab Podcast and associated research, Stanford University School of Medicine.*

Core insight: *Pioneering summaries of the aMCC and how voluntary effort callouses the will to endure and sustains high-level focus under pressure.*

Dweck, Carol S. *Mindset: The New Psychology of Success.* Stanford University / Random House.

Core insight: *The psychological foundation for why the Hard is necessary for neuroplasticity and growth. The growth mindset is not an attitude. It is a biological orientation toward productive difficulty.*

Duckworth, Angela. *Grit: The Power of Passion and Perseverance.* Scribner.

Core insight: *Empirical evidence that grit is a stronger predictor of success than IQ across high-stakes environments, and that grit is built through voluntary sustained effort.*

3. Polyvagal Theory and Autonomic Coherence

To lead a room, you must first lead your own nervous system.

Porges, Stephen W. *The Polyvagal Theory: Neurophysiological Foundations of Emotions, Attachment, Communication, and Self-Regulation.* W. W. Norton.

Core insight: *The discovery of the Social Engagement System and how the vagus nerve governs whether leaders and their teams are in a state of creativity or survival.*

Dana, Deb. *The Polyvagal Theory in Therapy: Engaging the Rhythm of Regulation.* W. W. Norton.

Core insight: *Practical applications of Porges' work, specifically regarding co-regulation and how one nervous system can stabilize another.*

McCraty, Rollin. *Science of the Heart.* HeartMath Institute.

Core insight: *Detailed research on Heart Rate Variability and autonomic coherence as measurable metrics for emotional intelligence and leadership presence.*

4. Human Performance and the Hard Path

The evidence base for how physical ordeals and environmental friction translate into cognitive and longevity dividends.

Easter, Michael. *The Comfort Crisis: Embrace Discomfort to Reclaim Your Wild, Happy, Healthy Self.* Rodale Books.

Core insight: *The anthropological and biological evidence for why modern ease is undermining human resilience, and why structured discomfort (the Misogi) is a prerequisite for a meaningful life.*

Goggins, David. *Can't Hurt Me: Master Your Mind and Defy the Odds.*

Core insight: *The Calloused Mind theory: a case study in aMCC growth through sheer voluntary effort. Extreme in method, rigorous in result.*

Levine, Peter A. *Waking the Tiger: Healing Trauma.* North Atlantic Books.

Core insight: *The mechanism of neurogenic tremoring as a biological reset: how the body discharges accumulated stress through involuntary physical release. The scientific context for what happened at mile 140.*

Van der Kolk, Bessel. *The Body Keeps the Score*. Viking.

Core insight: *The physiological storage of emotional armor and the body's role in identity. The biological argument for why cognitive-only approaches to leadership development fail.*

Stair Climbing and Longevity Research: Various studies published in the *British Journal of Sports Medicine* and the *European Society of Cardiology*. Core finding: 24% reduction in all-cause mortality and 39% reduction in cardiovascular death associated with consistent stair climbing as a daily micro-ordeal.

5. Digital Ethics and Attention

Why severance is a prerequisite for sovereignty in a hyper-connected world.

Newport, Cal. *Deep Work: Rules for Focused Success in a Distracted World*. Grand Central Publishing.

Core insight: *The concept of Attention Residue and the economic necessity of protecting the prefrontal cortex from the Digital Fog. The cognitive case for scheduled disconnection.*

Lanier, Jaron. *Ten Arguments for Deleting Your Social Media Accounts Right Now*. Henry Holt.

Core insight: *The philosophical and ethical dangers of algorithmic manipulation and the erosion of human agency. The case for digital sovereignty as an ethical position, not just a productivity strategy.*

This bibliography reflects sources cited or substantively referenced throughout HARD: Building Your Inner Citadel. Where podcast episodes are cited (Huberman Lab), the relevant episode is noted in the chapter-level references. Full academic citations available on request.

www.ingramcontent.com/pod-product-compliance
Lightning Source LLC
LaVergne TN
LVHW010609110826
845149LV00003B/837
9798995659112